Managing Hypertension

Managing Hypertension

THE COMPLETE PROGRAM DEVELOPED BY
THE CLEVELAND CLINIC

James V. Warren, M.D.
and Genell J. Subak-Sharpe

DOUBLEDAY & COMPANY, INC.

GARDEN CITY, NEW YORK

1986

Library of Congress Cataloging in Publication Data

Warren, James V. (James Vaughn), 1915–
Managing hypertension.
1. Hypertension. 2. Self-care, Health.
I. Subak-Sharpe, Genell J. II. Cleveland Clinic.
III. Title. [DNLM: 1. Hypertension—therapy.
2. Self Care. WG 340 W289c]
RC685.H8W36 1986   616.1'32   85-15968
ISBN 0-385-18768-8

Dedication

In deep appreciation to Dr. Irvine Page and all the other medical pioneers who have contributed so much to the management of hypertension.

Acknowledgments

Scores of people have worked with us to make this book a reality. While it is not possible to recognize all of them, there are some whose contributions cannot be overlooked. These include many Cleveland Clinic Foundation physicians, researchers, and other staff members, most notably Drs. Ray W. Gifford, Jr., Donald G. Vidt, Robert C. Tarazi, and Fetnat M. Fouad. Helen Brown, Ph.D., has been invaluable in providing dietary information, including recipes. Veronica Hiebel, Frank Weaver, Marion Mosley, and Irene Chang have lent background material and pointed us in the right direction for gathering information. Special thanks are due the Cleveland Clinic patients who shared their experiences with us.

Emily Paulsen and Diane Goetz have seen to many of the essential details in pulling together the final manuscript. The American Heart Association has been most generous in supplying data and background information. Our Doubleday editors Loretta Barrett and Cynthia Barrett and copy editor Glenn Rounds deserve a special tribute for their patience and sensitive editing.

Finally, a very special tribute is due our respective families. Our spouses, Gloria Warren and Gerald Subak-Sharpe, have reviewed the manuscript and filled in important gaps. David, Sarah, and Hope Subak-Sharpe have pitched in to help with typing, messengering, and extra understanding.

Contents

Introduction: The Cleveland Clinic's Role in the Modern Treatment of Hypertension

This book provides a comprehensive overview of one of our most common—and most serious—diseases, hypertension or high blood pressure. It is also the story of a triumph of medical science. One hundred years ago, no one knew about hypertension. Doctors did not measure blood pressure, nor did they relate it to strokes, heart attacks, kidney failure, blindness, and other outcomes of the disease.

Medicine has advanced on virtually every front in these last hundred years. The serious consequences of high blood pressure are now well known. But as recently as forty years ago, we lacked the tools to really treat the disease. Franklin Delano Roosevelt died of malignant hypertension, a rapidly progressive form of the disease that was once relatively common and inevitably fatal. Today, malignant hypertension is so unusual that it is almost a medical curiosity.

In the last decade or so, physicians and patients alike have become more aware of hypertension. Only ten or fifteen years ago, most doctors did not bother to routinely measure a patient's blood pressure; today, most doctors include a blood pressure measurement in all office visits. Millions of heretofore undetected hypertensives have been identified and brought under treatment, thanks to this increased diligence.

Of course, there are still many unanswered questions. Why do so many people have high blood pressure when there are no other signs of disease? For some patients, a cause for the high blood pressure can be found, but in the large majority, it is truly a "silent disease" that can smolder for twenty years or more before making itself apparent. By that time, the heart, brain, blood vessels, kidneys, and eyes—the major "target organs" of hypertension—may have incurred permanent damage.

There is no cure for the vast majority of hypertensive patients; their treatment must be lifelong. While this may seem a dismal prospect, the good news is that lifelong treatment means a longer, more productive life. A patient with hypertension truly forms a partnership with his or her doctor in managing the disease. In this book, you will meet several Cleveland Clinic patients. When talking to these patients, we were struck by their terminology. None said "the doctor did this or that"; instead, they described how "we tried this combination of treatments" or "when that didn't work, we went on to the next step." This is what the treatment of high blood pressure is all about. To make it work, the patient needs to be educated because it is the patient who day by day administers the treatment. The doctor is there to review the results and make suggestions, but true blood pressure control rests with the patient.

In this book, we present the Cleveland Clinic's approach to hypertension. As with all of the Frontiers in Medicine books, we focus on an institution that has developed a prototypical program. For the last fifty years, the Cleveland Clinic has been at the forefront of hypertension treatment, research, and education. This does not imply that there are not other institutions where patients can get exemplary medical care for this disease; today, there are hundreds of clinics, institutions, and physicians who offer excellent care to hypertensive patients. But a good deal of our understanding of the modern treatment of hypertension, as well as the development of the first antihypertensive agents, have their roots in early research and patient care at the Cleveland Clinic. It is still one of the leading centers that physicians around the world refer their most difficult cases to.

The Cleveland Clinic was founded in 1921 by four physicians as a non-profit group medical practice. It has since become one of the world's largest privately funded medical centers, dedicated to "better care of the sick, further study of their problems, and more teaching of those who serve." The Clinic now occupies a rapidly expanding complex of buildings located on a fifty-acre campus in the heart of Cleveland. It has more than five hundred full-time physicians and about an equal number of residents and other physician trainees. More than a half million patients visit the Cleveland Clinic each year, coming from almost every state of the union and seventy-two foreign countries. It is especially known for its open-heart surgery—the first coronary bypass operation was performed here—but the Clinic has a reputation for excellence in many different areas of medicine.

In cataloging the many accomplishments of the Cleveland Clinic, one keeps coming back to the hypertension saga and the researcher who ushered in the modern era of antihypertensive therapy. That man was Dr. Irvine Page, who was one of the first to correlate high blood pressure with strokes, heart attacks, and kidney failure—three of the most lethal consequences of untreated hypertension.

Dr. Page was born in Indianapolis, Indiana, on January 7, 1901. He has devoted all of his adult life to medicine, and continues to write, think about, and participate in this field, though he is eighty-five and has officially retired to Cape Cod.

After earning a bachelor's degree in chemistry at Cornell University in 1921, he went on to the Cornell University Medical School, graduating in 1926. Following a two-year internship at New York's Presbyterian Hospital, he became head of the chemical division of the Kaiser Wilhelm Institute in Munich. At one time, he considered becoming a German citizen, but with the rise of Hitler, he knew that hard times lay ahead and he returned to the United States to take a research position at the Rockefeller Institute for Medical Research (now Rockefeller University). He stayed there until 1937, then returned to his home city of Indianapolis to become director of the laboratory for clinical research at the Indianapolis City Hospital. At the end of World War II, he was appointed director of the Research Division of the Cleveland Clinic. By that time, he had formulated many of his basic concepts about hypertension, but it was not until 1949 that he published his landmark "mosaic theory," in which he postulated that a number of factors —genetic, environmental, anatomical, adaptive, neural, endocrine, humoral, and hemodynamic—all intertwine to raise blood pressure.

From the beginning, Dr. Page held that blood pressure was a part of the body's wondrously "calibrated system that maintains itself without destroying itself. It must adjust constantly to harsh climates and all the other things that assail us."

At the Cleveland Clinic, Dr. Page set about to organize a broadly based program ranging from fundamental chemistry to practical clinical applications. He gathered together many of the leading researchers and clinicians in the field. They studied the roles of different body chemicals and, for the first time, achieved insight into some of the basic controls of blood pressure. Their work in the laboratory was paralleled by advances in patient care. The first patient to be effectively treated with an antihypertensive drug was at the Cleveland Clinic—his dramatic story is told in this book. Some of the work started thirty to forty years ago by Dr. Page and his colleagues is only now bearing fruit in the introduction of new antihypertensive drugs.

The work is by no means finished. Many of the young scientists trained by Dr. Page are now at other institutions, still working to unravel the mystery of hypertension. Many are still at the Cleveland Clinic, and they have been joined by new researchers.

"We have come a long way in the last forty years," says Dr. Robert Tarazi, Vice Chairman of the Research Division and Head of the Cleveland Clinic's Clinical Science Department. "But in some areas, we are only beginning. For example, we still know very little about the role of the brain in hypertension. Until recently, we thought that the heart was only a target organ of the disease and that once there was cardiac hypertrophy [enlargement of the heart], the damage was irreversible. We are now beginning to realize that these assumptions are not necessarily true; the heart may be an instigator as well as a target organ. With early and proper treatment, some cardiac hypertrophy can be reversed. These are exciting discoveries that open whole new areas of thought and investigation."

The excitement is almost infectious. It involves not only the researchers but also the physicians and patients. We have tried to capture some of that excitement in this book, in addition to presenting the most up-to-date information on the diagnosis and treatment of hypertension.

1
High Blood Pressure: Defining the Problem

High blood pressure or hypertension, to use its medical name, is one of the most common and most serious diseases afflicting Americans. The American Heart Association estimates that more than thirty-seven million people—or about one out of every four adults in this country—have high blood pressure. Some experts put the figure even higher. For example, the Joint National Committee on Detection, Evaluation, and Treatment of High Blood Pressure—a part of the National High Blood Pressure Education Program—estimates that there are sixty million Americans with high blood pressure.

Tragically, many of these hypertensives do not know they are walking around with a potentially life-threatening disease. The Heart Association estimates that there are eighteen million Americans with high blood pressure who do not know they have hypertension. Even among those who know they have high blood pressure, about half either drop out of treatment or are being inadequately treated. Although this is actually better than a decade ago, the fact that nearly 50 percent of all people with an established diagnosis of hypertension still have higher than normal blood pressure clearly means that a greater effort must be made to educate people about this disease.

The consequences of untreated hypertension are often lethal. High blood pressure is directly responsible for about thirty-two thousand deaths in the United States each year, but its toll is much higher. Hypertension is also a major factor in heart attacks, strokes and, to a lesser degree, kidney failure. It can cause blindness and hardening of the arteries. In all, experts estimate that it is a cause, either direct or indirect, in more than a million deaths a year.

In addition to being one of our most lethal diseases, high blood pressure is also one of our most expensive. Conservative estimates put its cost at more than fifteen billion dollars a year. When time lost from work and other costs are added to it, the total economic burden is much higher.

Although these facts are grim, there is a bright side. Hypertension is one disease that can almost always be effectively treated. In fact, advances in the diagnosis and treatment of hypertension over the last fifteen years are to a great extent responsible for a dramatic 45 percent reduction in deaths from strokes since 1970. Similarly, the death toll from heart attacks has dropped by 25 percent, a figure that is particularly important since this is our number one cause of death. The mortality from kidney failure has also declined. Although the reasons for these declines are not completely clear, most experts agree that the development of more effective treatments of hypertension deserves a good share of the credit. What's more, today's approaches to diagnosis and treatment are more exact than in the past, meaning that an ever-increasing number of patients can bring their blood pressures under control without suffering unpleasant or debilitating side effects.

In this book, we focus on the pioneering approaches to hypertension at the Cleveland Clinic, the institution where modern antihypertensive therapy was born. The approaches described here are now widely available throughout the United States. Ongoing research at the Cleveland Clinic and elsewhere is constantly producing new understanding of this disease. With increased understanding come even more effective treatments. The basic purpose of this book is to help you understand what is involved in controlling high blood pressure—why it is so important and why only you, working as an informed partner with your doctor, can maintain normal blood pressure. Myths and misconceptions about high blood pressure abound; these can be countered only with facts and understanding. We will also offer practical advice on what you should—and should not—eat, on how you should exercise, and tips on how to cope with stress. Above all, it is important to remember that a diagnosis of hypertension can mark a new beginning; the disease still does not have a cure—except in those unusual instances where a cause can be identified and eliminated—but it is by no means an automatic death sentence. Most people with hypertension can be effectively treated and live normal, productive lives. Our goal is to show you how.

At the outset, it should be noted that there is no one treatment for hypertension. Doctors still do not fully agree as to when antihypertensive treatment should be started or what it should entail. Many factors, such as age, evidence of organ damage from the high blood pressure, and, of course, the level of blood pressure itself, are among the considerations in designing a treatment program. In addition, the treatment protocols are constantly being revised with the introduction of new drugs and the accumulation of new data. This book represents the latest thinking among experts at the Cleveland Clinic and elsewhere, and it is based on decades of experience in treating the disease. But ongoing research may well alter this knowledge in ways that cannot be anticipated.

WHAT IS HIGH BLOOD PRESSURE?

Blood pressure and its regulation is a complex process that involves a number of different organ systems, all working in concert. The human body has an extraordinarily efficient network of blood vessels, totaling some sixty thousand miles. The largest of these vessels, the great arteries, measure about four fifths of an inch in diameter. The smallest are barely visible, with a diameter of .0004 of an inch.

When we speak of blood pressure, we are referring to the force that flowing blood exerts against the artery walls. The veins also have pressure within them, but it is at a much lower level and, so far as hypertension is concerned, it is of little consequence.

In order to live, each cell of the body must have a steady supply of blood to bring oxygen and other nutrients and to carry away carbon dioxide and other waste materials. In a sense, the cardiovascular system serves as a plumbing system to deliver blood to all parts of the body and collect and carry away wastes. The average adult has about eleven pints of blood, which constantly circulates through the body. About seventy times a minute, the heart contracts or beats, forcing about two to three ounces of blood from its pumping chamber—the left ventricle—into the aorta. This is the largest artery in the body; branching off from it are numerous smaller arteries, which in turn branch again and again into ever smaller vessels, ending up as the arterioles. These are the body's smallest arteries; they also have the greatest portion of smooth muscle in their walls. Contraction and relaxation of these muscles regulates the flow of blood to each organ system. In effect, the arterioles act something like the faucets in a plumbing system. They control the amount of blood flow and the pressure, or force, with which it moves through the area being nourished by it.

Although the force required to keep blood moving through the body originates in the heart, many other organ systems are involved in coordinating the many responses that maintain and monitor blood pressure. To envision how this works, imagine that the body has a number of control mechanisms whose major function is to maintain blood pressure, just as a thermostat maintains and controls the heat in a room. Some of these mechanisms go into action to compensate for sudden changes or demands on the cardiovascular system, such as when you suddenly stand up or exercise. Without a mechanism that can quickly adjust to the change in position or need for blood, you faint. To prevent this, the various pressure thermostats adjust the amount of blood that is flowing through the body, either by increasing the heartbeat or the amount of blood that is pumped with each beat, or by altering the size of the arterioles, as a means of maintaining the desired blood pressure.

A common theory holds that hypertension is a disease characterized by a malfunctioning "thermostat." Just as a room becomes too warm if a thermostat is set too high, some bodily processes may result in the blood pressure thermostatic controls being set at too high a level. This seems to be the case in primary, or essential, hypertension. Most people with primary hypertension have no symptoms nor obvious cause of their high blood pressure; the control mechanisms are working properly to compensate for changes in posture, physical activity, and so forth, but in a significant number of people, these controls are set too high.

When individual blood pressure measurements are studied scientifically and plotted out, we have a range that produces a bell-shaped curve, typical of a normal distribution, with a few people at the extreme upper and lower ends but most people falling somewhere in the middle. Until recent years, physicians and researchers disagreed as to whether primary hypertension is at the high end of a normal curve, or is it a disease? Most experts now agree that persistent blood pressure above a certain level is, indeed, a disease, although it is one that many people live with without symptoms for twenty years or more. Still, this persistent high blood pressure does take its toll, and there is little doubt that it leads to premature death. There also is little doubt that lowering it is a major step in preventing death and disability from strokes, heart attacks, and kidney failure.

A MULTIFACTORIAL DISEASE

It is increasingly apparent that hypertension is a complex, multifactorial disease caused by an interaction of a number of body systems or mechanisms rather than a failure of just one. Three systems, each with a variety of thermostatic sensors, control the blood vessels: the kidney; the autonomic nervous system, which governs automatic or involuntary responses and functions, such as the heartbeat; and the adrenal glands, which secrete the stress hormones epinephrine and norepinephrine and the steroid hormones (aldosterone, cortisone, and others) that help control the body's balance of salt and water, as well as metabolism.

The most important of the thermostatic sensors is perhaps the carotid sinus, a pressure-sensitive part of the autonomic nervous system that is located in the major artery carrying blood to the brain. Obviously, the brain requires a steady and reliable blood supply. If this supply is threatened, there is an almost instantaneous response that raises blood pressure and increases the heart rate as well as the amount of blood being pumped by it. Other sensors, such as those in the kidneys, are instrumental in maintaining blood pressure over a longer period by controlling the amount of fluid circulating in the body.

Hormones also play an important role in regulating blood pressure. The stress hormones, epinephrine and norepinephrine, are released by the adrenal medulla in response to a threat to the body. Epinephrine is a powerful stimulant that makes the heart beat faster; norepinephrine is a vasoconstrictor, meaning that it causes the muscles in the blood vessels to constrict, thus raising blood pressure. By increasing blood pressure and the heart rate, these hormones prepare the body for a fight-or-flight reaction to danger. The steroid hormones are important in maintaining the body's salt and water balance. By conserving salt, the body's fluid level is increased, resulting in an increased blood volume. Faced with more blood to circulate, the heart and blood vessels respond by raising blood pressure.

In recent years, researchers have intensified their study of the role of renin, a substance secreted by kidneys, in controlling blood pressure. Renin was first identified in 1898 when researchers found that it raised the blood pressure in animals. Subsequent studies, conducted primarily at the Cleveland Clinic, found that renin alone does not do this. Instead, the Clinic's famed researcher, Dr. Irvine Page, discovered that it produces a hormone called angiotensin, which causes the muscles in the blood vessels to constrict, thereby narrowing the vessels.

Angiotensin also stimulates the release of another hormone, aldosterone, from the adrenal cortex. This hormone, which is one of the steroids, also affects blood pressure. This renin-angiotension-aldosterone system is highly sensitive to any change in blood pressure. Even a minute drop in pressure will stimulate the kidneys to release renin and set the cycle in motion. The major effect is an increase in blood volume, brought about by an increased retention of water. When the fall in blood pressure is countered, the kidneys stop producing renin and blood volume returns to normal. But this does not always happen. For example, if one of the renal arteries, the major blood vessels that bring blood to the kidneys, is diseased or narrowed, the kidney will keep producing renin. The result is renovascular hypertension, a form of high blood pressure that can very quickly progress to malignant hypertension if a normal blood supply is not restored to the kidney or the diseased kidney is not removed.

Under other circumstances, the importance of renin is still not fully understood. While it is clear that malignant hypertension may develop if renin production is not shut off in renovascular hypertension, there is some disagreement among experts as to whether chronic excessive renin production unrelated to kidney disease is a factor in the much more common primary hypertension.

The heart itself may play a role in the development of hypertension. Traditionally, the heart is viewed as a victim of high blood pressure, but some researchers, such as Dr. Robert Tarazi of the Cleveland Clinic, believe that it also may play a part in the development of the disease. The brain is still another organ that is being studied by researchers at the Cleveland Clinic and elsewhere as a possible instigator of hypertension.

SYSTOLIC AND DIASTOLIC BLOOD PRESSURES

Blood does not flow through the arteries under a steady pressure, such as the flow of a river. Instead, it comes in spurts. The spurt, or wave-like surge in pressure, is created by the force of the heartbeat. The maximum force, which is exerted with each heartbeat, is called "systolic pressure." In between heartbeats, the pressure falls as the blood leaves the arterial systems and enters the capillaries—the microscopic vessels that nourish each cell—and then on to the veins, the vessels that return "used" blood to the heart and lungs for a fresh supply of oxygen. The lowest point of this resting phase between heartbeats is known as "diastolic pressure." This is why blood pressure is expressed in two numbers; ideally, 120/80. The higher number is the systolic pressure, the lower is the diastolic.

All blood vessels, but particularly those of the arterioles, are elastic, with muscles that cause them to dilate (open or widen), or constrict (close or narrow). This action is often likened to what happens in a garden hose. The smallest arteries, the arterioles, are instrumental in directing the flow of blood by dilating or constricting, just as a nozzle is instrumental in increasing or decreasing the amount of water from a hose, and can be used to decrease flow to one area and increase it to another. When you are exercising, for example, the arterioles to the muscles will dilate to increase the blood flow to them, while those supplying the stomach or other internal organs will constrict.

To envision how this works, imagine watering different parts of a flower garden. If the petunias are particularly dry, the nozzle of the hose serving that area of the garden will be opened to deliver more water. At the same time, the nozzle on the hoses serving the geraniums will be closed to reduce water flow there. Similarly, the body adjusts pressure within certain blood vessels to deliver blood to the parts of the body that need it most. The constriction of muscles within the vessels increases the resistance to the blood flow, similar to what happens when you tighten the nozzle on a garden hose, reducing the amount of water flowing through it.

These control systems are amazingly well coordinated, and most people are totally unaware of them. But they are not perfect. Sometimes a person will experience brief periods of dizziness or even faint when standing suddenly, a condition referred to as orthostatic hypotension. And, as we have seen, large numbers of people have their control system set too high, resulting in an average blood pressure that is too high.

MEASURING BLOOD PRESSURE

Although circulation has been studied for centuries, there is still a good deal that we do not know about its complex mechanisms. Until the early seventeenth century, it was not known that blood actually circulates through the body. In 1628, an English physician, William Harvey, described the concept of circulation in a landmark monograph entitled "De Motu Cordis et Sanguinis," which translated means "Concerning the Motion of the Heart and the Blood." As strange as it seems today, until Harvey's discovery, the relationship between the heart and the pulses was not appreciated, although Galileo and many earlier physicians and scientists had measured and studied pulse beats.

It took another century following Harvey's discovery to determine how to measure blood pressure. An English clergyman, the Reverend Stephen Hales, conducted experiments on living animals that demonstrated the existence of blood pressure. In his classic experiment, he measured the blood pressure of a horse while it was lying on its side. He placed a needle-like device into one of the horse's arteries, and through a flexible tube that was connected to a long glass tube, he found that the blood rose to a height of eight feet, three inches. He also noted that it rose and fell with the beating of the heart.

Over the last two hundred and fifty years, we have come a long way in our ability to measure blood pressure. Now the most accurate means of measuring arterial blood pressure is to insert a fine needle, or catheter, into an artery and to use electronic sensing devices and recorders to tell the blood pressure at any given moment. This is the method used to monitor blood pressure in a hospital critical care unit.

Obviously, these direct methods are complicated and require that an artery be punctured to measure blood pressure. Thus, we more commonly use an indirect way of measuring, utilizing an instrument called a sphygmomanometer. Although most of us have trouble spelling and pronouncing its name (sfig-moe-man-OM-a-ter), virtually all of us have had our blood pressure measured with it and it is simple enough to use at home with very little training. (See "Monitoring Your Own Blood Pressure," p. 148.)

In 1896, an Italian physician, Dr. Scipione Riva-Rocci, invented the portable sphygmomanometer, and his basic design is still used. The device has three parts: an inflatable rubber cuff, an air pump, and a column of mercury. Air is pumped into the inflatable cuff, which is wrapped firmly around the arm (a leg also can be used). The purpose is to determine how much pressure is needed to stop the flow of blood in the artery, because this is the same as the blood pressure. The rubber cuff is attached to a column of mercury. As the pressure in the cuff increases, it drives up the fluid in the column. Mercury is used because it is much heavier than water, and thus requires a relatively short tube—about eighteen inches compared to the nine feet that Stephen Hales needed when he used water to measure the blood pressure of a horse. Because the mercury manometer is still not as portable as some situations demand, the column of mercury has been replaced in some blood pressure machines by a device similar to an aneroid barometer. It is a thin metal bellows that expands with pressure and causes a needle to move on a dial. Blood pressure machines using these devices are compact and portable, making them easier for a doctor to carry around. Since they require periodic calibration and in a doctor's office or hospital setting, the mercury manometer remains the standard.

As air is pumped into the cuff and as the cuff tightens around the arm the pressure blocks blood flow beyond it. The cuff is then gradually decompressed. By using a stethoscope to listen to the sounds in the artery at a point below the cuff, you can hear a thumping sound as blood spurts through the partially opened artery. These are the sounds that were first described by a Russian physician, Dr. Nikolai Korotkoff, who found that listening to the pulse through a stethoscope was more accurate than feeling for its return with the fingers. By noting how high the mercury is when the first thumping sounds are heard, you can determine the systolic blood pressure. The cuff is then relaxed even more, which allows the artery to fully open. As the blood flow returns through the vessels, a different kind of sound is heard through the stethoscope. When these sounds disappear, blood flow has returned, and the level of mercury is again noted; this is the diastolic pressure. Thus the systolic reading is the amount of force exerted by a wave of blood as it leaves the heart, and the diastolic is the amount of resistance it must overcome to pass through the blood vessels. The two numbers in a blood pressure reading are millimeters of mercury, abbreviated as 120/80 mm Hg. In common parlance, however, blood pressure is usually referred to simply as 120 over 80, and written as 120/80.

THE MEANING OF BLOOD PRESSURE

As we have seen, blood pressure is subject to many controls and is not a steady flow but, instead, a series of wave-like spurts. Even these spurts are in a constant state of change. Hundreds of factors can cause a change in blood pressure. Like most body systems, blood pressure seems to have its own internal "clock." Generally, it is lowest when we are asleep; studies have found that, in most people, blood pressure falls to its lowest level in the predawn hours and is its highest in the first two or three hours after waking. But there may be scores of peaks and valleys at different times during the day. A sudden startle, such as a near fall or the sound of a car backfiring, can cause a momentary rise in blood pressure. Relaxing in a warm bath or meditating usually lowers it. Running to catch a bus, climbing a flight of stairs, rising to a standing position, arguing with a spouse or boss—all may produce a temporary rise in blood pressure. Very often, having blood pressure measured in a doctor's office produces an unexplained rise and sometimes may result in an unjustified diagnosis of hypertension.

These moment-to-moment fluctuations tend to be temporary and are not a cause of concern. But when the resting or basal blood pressure is consistently high, as evidenced from several measurements taken at different times and perhaps in different settings, there is reason to worry. People whose blood pressures are consistently high when resting also experience ups and downs, but these too are at a higher-than-normal level. Sustained high blood pressure damages the blood vessels and promotes arteriosclerosis, a "hardening" of the arteries that leads to a reduction in blood flow to vital organs, including the heart, brain, and kidneys.

Hypertension is often referred to as the "silent killer" because it usually does not produce symptoms until considerable damage has been done. But the consequences of long-term untreated hypertension are well known. For example, hypertension is a major cause of heart disease. High blood pressure causes the heart to work harder. After years of excessive pumping action, the heart muscle becomes thick, leading to an enlarged, less effective heart. High blood pressure also damages the coronary arteries, the blood vessels that encircle the heart and provide its nourishment. Damaged, clogged coronary arteries are the major cause of the one and a half million heart attacks that afflict Americans each year and result in 550,000 deaths.

Untreated hypertension is the leading cause of strokes. Although there has been a marked decline in strokes over the last fifteen years, there are still a half million each year, with a death toll of more than 164,000. In addition, there are nearly two million living Americans who have survived strokes but have suffered varying degrees of disability. A stroke may occur when a weakened blood vessel ruptures in the brain or, more commonly, when a clot forms in an already narrowed artery, blocking blood flow to that part of the brain. The effects of the strokes—for example, paralysis on one side of the body or speech difficulties—depend upon the part of the brain that has been damaged.

The kidney is still another vital organ that is damaged by high blood pressure. Since the kidney is the body's major filter, it receives more blood flow than other organs. When long-term hypertension damages the tiny blood vessels of the kidney, progressive renal failure may result.

Excessive blood pressure also may damage the tiny blood vessels of the eye, leading to hemorrhages and eventual loss of vision. This is particularly common among people with diabetes who also have high blood pressure—two diseases that often occur together. The eyes also provide an index of how much damage blood vessels elsewhere in the body may suffer from the hypertension. When a doctor looks into eyes, any changes such as a narrowing of the blood vessels, swelling or buildup of fluid, or accumulation of debris in the eye chamber will be noted. The more damage noted to these vessels, the more likely there is to be damage to the kidney and other so-called target organs.

The adverse effects of hypertension are magnified when it occurs along with other diseases or life-style habits that promote disease. For example, an overweight hypertensive who smokes and has high levels of blood cholesterol is much more likely to suffer a heart attack or die prematurely than a person who has only one of these risk factors. Still, hypertension alone lowers overall life expectancy. Life insurance studies have found that a thirty-five-year-old man with untreated hypertension does not enjoy the same life expectancy as a comparable man with normal blood pressure. The degree of risk is related to the level of blood pressure. Those who fall into the category of mild to moderate hypertension lose three to six years from their normal life expectancy, and with even higher blood pressure (i.e., 180/100), the loss may go up to eight years (see Table 1.1 on p. 15).

HOW HIGH IS TOO HIGH?

Doctors still disagree over what constitutes hypertension and at what level treatment should be instituted. Everyone agrees that consistent resting blood pressure readings of 120/80 are absolutely normal, even though most people do not have 120/80 every time their blood pressures are measured. But an average at or near this figure is the ideal goal. A reading as low as 70/50 in a baby or as high as 135 or 140/85 in a healthy adult also are in the normal range.

Both systolic and diastolic readings are important, but traditionally the diastolic pressure has been emphasized more than the systolic. Studies have found that sustained diastolic readings of 85 increase the risk of a heart

TABLE 1.1. LIFE EXPECTANCY FOR HYPERTENSIVES

AGE—35 YEARS

MAN

Blood Pressure Levels	Life Expectancy*	Years Lost†
Normal	39.1	—
140/90	36.1	3.0
160/95	33.1	6.0
180/100	31.1	8.0

WOMAN

Normal	45.0	—
140/90	43.0	2.0
160/95	41.0	4.0
180/100	39.5	5.5

AGE—65 YEARS

MAN

Normal	14.5	—
140/90	12.5	2.0
160/95	10.5	4.0
180/100	9.5	5.0

WOMAN

Normal	18.8	—
140/90	17.3	1.5
160/95	15.8	3.0
180/100	14.8	4.0

* Life expectancies taken from the American Council of Life Insurance *Fact Book,* 1984, p. 93.
† Years of life lost due to hypertension taken from Edward A. Lew, "Treatment of Hypertension," in *Transactions of the Association of Life Insurance Medical Directors of America, Eighty-ninth Annual Meeting,* vol. LXIV, 1981, p. 127. Mr. Lew is a retired Vice President and Actuary, Metropolitan Life Insurance Company.

attack, stroke, or other consequences of hypertension and should be either treated or carefully monitored. Dr. Ray W. Gifford, Jr., Chairman of the Cleveland Clinic's Department of Hypertension and Nephrology, and his colleagues define diastolic blood pressures of 85 to 90 as "high normal," and deserving of careful monitoring and perhaps conservative treatment. Although more attention is usually paid to the diastolic reading than to the systolic, Dr. Gifford notes that the latter actually may be the more important prognosticator of a heart attack.

People whose diastolic pressures are in the 90 to 94 range are in a gray area of mild hypertension. Some doctors think that monitoring and life-style changes, such as losing excessive weight, stopping smoking, restricting salt, and increasing exercise are sufficient. Others, including physicians at the Cleveland Clinic, think that there is enough risk to justify a more aggressive approach. If life-style changes do not lower the diastolic readings to 90 or less in six months, antihypertensive drugs may be prescribed.

Diastolic pressures in the 95–99 range also may be treated initially by life-style modification, but antihypertensive drugs may be prescribed if a lowering has not occurred in three to six months. Most doctors now agree that consistent diastolic readings of 100 or higher justify starting drug therapy to lower the blood pressure. (Treatment of high blood pressure is discussed in more detail in chapters 4 through 12.)

In summary, there is still much that is unknown about blood pressure, and what causes it to rise in some people and stay normal in others. It is obvious that many body systems and controls are involved, both in the genesis of hypertension and as target organs of its damage. Not all doctors agree as to the best way to treat hypertension, but a large number of studies conducted over the last twenty years involving many thousands of patients make it clear that lowering even mild high blood pressure reduces the risk of premature death from a heart attack or stroke. There are now dozens of effective drugs that lower high blood pressure, and either a single drug or a combination of several agents can be found for almost all patients to control their hypertension without intolerable side effects.

2
Who Gets High Blood Pressure?

Although there are many stereotypes of people with hypertension, the fact is there is no such thing as a "typical hypertensive." Hypertension affects all social and economic classes. It can occur in children as well as older people. Men and women both develop it, as do people of all racial backgrounds. This great diversity is apparent in visiting with patients who are "regulars" in the Cleveland Clinic's hypertension section.

Mrs. Olds (not her real name) is a fifty-seven-year-old Cleveland writer and musician who was first diagnosed as having high blood pressure when she was in her early thirties, although she suspects the disease was present long before that. "I have always had a weight problem," she recalls, "even as a child. After college, I went to Mexico to work with a motion picture producer. I also wrote the bull-fighting column for a newspaper in Mexico City.

"It was a very tense, high-pressure time in my life, and I had a lot of health problems at that time. But no one ever diagnosed the problem as high blood pressure. It was not until I returned to the United States and became pregnant for the first time that I had a problem with high blood pressure. I developed toxemia and lost the baby. I have had high blood pressure ever since."

Although Mrs. Olds now appears to be a model of good health and leads an involved, active life, she has had a number of serious health problems in the last twenty years, most of them related to her blood pressure, which was a very high 210/160. In 1969, she suffered her first heart attack, followed by two more heart attacks and progressive coronary artery disease. "I finally underwent bypass surgery in 1983," she explains, "and that has made a big difference." In the last three years, her diabetes has progressed to the point where she now needs insulin injections. But since her coronary bypass surgery, she has lost more than thirty pounds and finds she feels better and is much more active than before.

"My husband and I joined a health club and I swim for almost an hour every day or so," she explains. Walking is difficult for Mrs. Olds because she has circulatory problems in her legs. "I feel better than I have for years," she says, ascribing her present well-being to her treatment regimen and her altered life-style. "At one time, I was taking thirty pills a day," she recalls, "but now I'm down to four different drugs plus the insulin."

Mrs. Olds is a good example of someone who has mastered living with serious diseases without giving up or letting the illnesses take an upper hand.

Miss Youngman is a forty-nine-year-old medical secretary who learned she has hypertension in 1979. At that time, her blood pressure was 210/110. Since she works in the medical world, she knew immediately that she had a potentially serious disease. "When the doctors told me that I was going to have to take medication, I was determined to be a 'good' patient." She takes her antihypertensive drugs religiously, and her blood pressure is stabilized at 160/85 or 90. "I get very concerned when it hits 90," she says. In addition to taking her antihypertensive medication, she has cut back on salt and fatty foods. "The one thing I haven't been able to do is give up smoking," she confesses, "but that's next on my list."

Miss Youngman's quiet determination in managing her disease is reflected in other areas of her life. "I had never worked before, so when I went out looking for a job in 1963, the only thing I could find was at the bottom of the ladder." She began in the hospital laundry and, over the years, has worked her way up to a secretarial position. "I am very determined," she says, "and I suppose you could describe me as a hyper Type A. This may have some effect on my blood pressure. I was naturally very worried and upset when I was first diagnosed, but I am just as determined not to let it get me down. I know what I have to do, and I do it. So far, it has worked well."

Mr. Rhodes also has a long history of high blood pressure. "I was rejected for the draft when I was twenty-one because my blood pressure was high," he says. "Over the years, my family doctor would take my blood pressure from time to time, but he never seemed very concerned." It wasn't until he took an insurance physical in 1969 and was told that his blood pressure was quite high that he sought treatment. "My father had high blood pressure and died of a heart attack when he was fifty. My mother also had high blood pressure, and most of the other members of my family have it. So I knew that I was at special risk."

Mr. Rhodes underwent coronary bypass surgery in 1973. He takes four different antihypertensive drugs. "Taking all these drugs is not pleasant," he says, "and I have had depression and sex problems that are probably related to the drugs. These have created some difficult times in my life, but I've learned to cope. After all, look at the alternatives."

Mrs. Blake is another Cleveland Clinic patient who is a good example of someone who has learned to live with a disease. Now sixty-eight years old, she first learned she had high blood pressure nearly forty years ago. This was before the era of modern antihypertensive drugs, so she was put on a low-salt weight reduction diet. "I was obese," she recalls, "and first went to a doctor about my weight problem. At that time, I found out I had high blood pressure." She now takes five different drugs and a total of nine or ten pills a day. "Some people ask how I can take all those pills, but I know that if I don't take the medication, I start to feel bad."

Like so many people, Mrs. Blake finds diet more difficult than taking pills. "I know what I should eat, and I do try," she says. "But I have a fatal weakness for ice cream. I shouldn't let ice cream in the house, but if it's in the refrigerator, I eat it."

Salt reduction is another problem for Mrs. Blake. "Food doesn't taste right without salt, but I'm learning better ways of cooking and using other seasonings instead of salt."

Now retired from her teaching job, Mrs. Blake says she misses the stimulation and activity of being around young children. "I keep busy taking care of the house and sewing. I also do volunteer work in schools and hospitals, but it's not the same as going to a job every day."

Although there is a certain pattern to these real-life stories, they also emphasize the popular misconceptions about who develops hypertension. The stereotype of the beefy, quick-tempered, red-faced male hypertensive is a popular example. People also tend to correlate hypertension with stress-ridden jobs or life-styles or a "nervous" personality, perhaps because of the presence of "tension" in the name of the disease. When used in this sense, tension does not refer to emotional stress or nervousness; instead, it describes the state of the blood vessels. Stress causes a temporary rise in blood pressure, but the mechanism by which it may cause the disease is unknown.

FACTORS THAT INCREASE THE ODDS

Recognizing that there are no "typical" hypertensives, it also should be noted that there are groups of people who are more susceptible to the disease than others. About 90 percent of all people with high blood pressure have primary hypertension. Also referred to as "essential hypertension," this form of the disease has no identifiable cause for the increased blood pressure. The remaining 10 percent of patients have secondary hypertension. In these patients, the high blood pressure has an identifiable cause, and in some cases, treating the underlying cause will cure the hypertension. One of the most common causes of secondary hypertension is kidney disease. Sometimes a renal blood vessel is blocked and the kidney responds to the reduced blood flow by producing renin, which sets in motion a mechanism to raise blood pressure. (Other causes of secondary hypertension are discussed in chapter 14.)

Although the causes of primary hypertension are unknown, a number of factors that increase its likelihood have been identified. These include:

HEREDITY

A family history of high blood pressure is a strong predisposing factor. Studies have found that children born to hypertensive parents often fall into the high-normal range, even at infancy. They remain at the high end of the scale and, very often, develop hypertension at an early age. Mr. Rhodes, one of the patients described earlier in this chapter, had a strong family history of hypertension on both sides of the family. Many experts now advocate that such people have their blood pressure checked regularly from an early age on, and take special precautions to modify or avoid other predisposing factors.

AGE

Hypertension sometimes occurs in childhood, but most often it develops in adults. Men tend to become hypertensive at an earlier age than women, but after the age of forty-five or fifty, women seem to "catch up" and the disease is evenly distributed between the sexes. Blood pressure tends to rise with age; what would be considered mild hypertension in a thirty-five- or forty-year-old may be acceptable, even though it is not normal, in a seventy-year-old.

RACIAL BACKGROUND

For reasons that are not clearly understood, blacks of all ages and both sexes are much more likely to have high blood pressure than whites. Some studies have found the incidence of hypertension among blacks two to three times that of comparable whites. Heredity is thought to play a role in this, although blacks in Africa do not seem to suffer hypertension in the high numbers as blacks in the United States. Some Oriental populations, notably the Japanese, also have a high incidence of hypertension.

OBESITY

Obesity increases the likelihood of hypertension. Studies have found that obese children who remain overweight are more likely to develop hypertension, and at an earlier age, than their normal weight peers. Very often, losing the excessive weight will lower the high blood pressure, especially if the weight reduction is accompanied by an increase in exercise.

SALT

Sodium along with potassium and chloride are essential electrolytes, which maintain the body's delicate balance of fluids, acids, and bases. All of our body tissues are bathed in salty water—this is thought to be a holdover from the early beginnings of life-forms on this planet. As we evolved from sea organisms, these early life-forms gradually adapted to life on the land. But they carried some of the sea with them in the form of the salty water that makes up most of the blood and other body fluids.

Sodium is essential because it helps the body retain the proper amount of fluid. When you eat salty foods, you feel thirsty and consume extra water to dilute the salt. The kidneys regulate the balance of sodium and fluids: when there is too much salt, the kidneys excrete it in the urine. When there is too little, salt is extracted from the urine and recirculated. In a certain type of high blood pressure, called volume-dependent hypertension, the body retains excessive sodium and there is an increase in blood volume.

In recent years, researchers have been studying the relationship between sodium and potassium and the possible role of potassium in protecting against hypertension. Again, let's look at our evolution for a possible explanation. Our prehistoric ancestors were foragers. Once they moved away from the sea, salt was scarce. They lived mostly on fruits, roots, grains, and other plant food—all good sources of potassium, but low in salt. To protect the body from sodium depletion, the kidneys developed an elaborate mechanism to conserve sodium and excrete potassium. We also developed a taste for salt.

Of course, in modern industrialized cultures, there's no shortage of salt and the dietary pattern is reversed. We tend to consume large amounts of salt while neglecting those foods that are high in potassium. We still have kidneys that are designed to conserve sodium and excrete potassium. "Some people are able to handle this salt overload," explains Dr. Louis Tobian, a researcher on hypertension at the University of Minnesota, "but people with a genetic susceptibility to hypertension probably cannot, resulting in high blood pressure and related problems."

A number of studies have implicated diet, specifically a high intake of salt and low intake of potassium, with an increased risk of hypertension, but it appears this is most true for people with a high genetic susceptibility for the disease.

In the early days of hypertension research, several population studies found that people who eat very little salt have little or no hypertension. Primitive societies in the Kalahari Desert, Kenya, the Amazon, and the Solomon Islands were studied and found that they consumed very little salt and also had no hypertension. But then other researchers noted that there are some population groups that eat large amounts of salt, for example, Eskimos in Alaska, and they also have a very low incidence of hypertension. Dr. Lewis Dahl, a researcher at the State University of New York at Stony Brook, set out to develop a laboratory animal model that would respond to salt in the same way as humans. He succeeded in breeding a strain of rats, which still are known as Dahl rats, that were genetically susceptible to develop hypertension when fed salt. If the rats were not given sodium, their blood pressures remained normal; but the littermates that were fed a high-salt diet developed very high blood pressure. The effect was not immediate, however; it usually took a month or so for the blood pressure to rise. Dr. Dahl postulated that the same thing happened in humans with a genetic trait for hypertension; the disease usually does not show up in childhood, but develops in the third or fourth decades.

Further studies with the Dahl rats found that their kidneys excreted about half as much salt as hypertension-resistant strains of animals. Why this is so is not known. Ongoing studies indicate it may be a combination of factors. Dr. Tobian and his colleagues have implicated several factors which may be interrelated. These include a reduction in production of prostaglandins, hormone-like substances with numerous functions, in the kidneys; the brain's response to a salt stimulus; and a possible deficiency of potassium. Explains Dr. Tobian: "We have found that if you feed a lot of potassium [to susceptible Dahl rats], it mitigates the hypertension-producing effect of salt on their kidneys."

In practical terms, population studies of some hypertension-prone groups in Japan, who eat about as much salt as the Eskimos and much more than the average American, have shown that if these Japanese are put on a low-salt diet at an early age, they are not as likely to become hypertensive later in life. While salt undoubtedly plays a role, most experts think that salt alone does not raise blood pressure. Still, since most people do not know whether they have a genetic predisposition to high blood pressure, cutting back on sodium is considered a good idea.

ORAL CONTRACEPTIVES

A small number of women who take the pill may develop high blood pressure, especially if they have a genetic disposition for hypertension. Women who already have high blood pressure are advised not to take the pill. Some physicians offer similar advice to women with a strong family history of the disease, or to women who are obese or who have had pregnancies complicated by hypertension. The pill also is not advised for women who smoke or who are over the age of forty. It should be noted that only a few of the millions of women who use oral contraceptives develop hypertension, and most of those do so in the first six months of use. Still, all women who use the pill should have their blood pressure checked regularly and should be aware of possible danger signs: excessive weight gain, puffy ankles or other signs of edema, blurred vision, headaches, and dizzy spells.

If hypertension does occur, the pill should be discontinued and an alternative method of birth control used. High blood pressure induced by the pill usually disappears within six months; if it does not, other means of treatment may be needed.

STRESS

Many people associate stress with hypertension, but medical evidence supporting this notion is lacking. Some studies have found that people in occupations with a particularly high stress level, for example, air traffic controllers, have a higher incidence of hypertension than people in less stressful jobs. But other studies have found that executives, whose jobs are commonly thought of as stressful, do not have as high an incidence of hypertension as laborers. Dr. Gifford notes that the incidence of hypertension also tends to be inversely related to the level of education—specifically, the higher the level of education, the lower the likelihood of developing high blood pressure. "But the reasons for these various associations are unknown and difficult to document," Dr. Gifford emphasizes. "A stressful situation may produce a transient rise in blood pressure, but it has not been proved that stress itself causes hypertension."

PERSONALITY TYPE

Since people respond to stress in different ways, researchers are also looking at the possible role of personality type in the development of hypertension. A number of studies have linked Type A personality, which is characterized by excessive attention to time, aggressiveness, and driving ambition, among other traits, to an increase in cardiovascular disease.

Recent studies have found that Type A people, especially those who tend to have high levels of anger and aggressiveness, release large amounts of stress hormones, even in situations in which they are not being challenged. These hormones raise blood pressure; the theory is that consistently high levels may produce hypertension. These people are referred to as "hyper" or "hot" reactors. Their blood pressure tends to bounce up and down frequently. Some are invariably hypertensive when their blood pressures are measured at work, for example, and normotensive at home or in other environments. They are sometimes referred to as "labile hypertensives," with normal blood pressures at some times and dangerously high spikes at others. There is some disagreement among doctors as to whether labile hypertension should be treated. A good deal depends upon individual circumstances and the presence of other risk factors. Generally, however, people with labile hypertension are advised to have their blood pressure checked regularly, perhaps including learning how to take it themselves at home. If it develops into chronic primary hypertension with elevated readings all or most of the time, treatment is then recommended.

OTHER LIFE-STYLE FACTORS

Cigarette smoking is probably the habit that is cited most as a life-style factor associated with cardiovascular disorders. There is no doubt that smoking a cigarette produces a temporary rise in blood pressure, but cigarette smoking does not lead to hypertension. Says Dr. Gifford: "Cigarette smoking is especially harmful for people with high blood pressure not because it increases the severity of the hypertension, but because it is an independent risk factor for the same things that hypertension is a risk factor for. In other words, smoking increases the risk of a heart attack and so does hypertension. Therefore, a hypertensive who smokes has an even greater risk of a heart attack than does a nonsmoking hypertensive."

A sedentary life-style is yet another factor that has been linked to an increased risk of hypertension. Aerobic exercise conditioning has been shown to produce a moderate lowering of blood pressure in mild hypertensives, but again, a number of other factors may be present that increase blood pressure. For example, a sedentary person is more likely to be overweight than someone who is physically active. It may be the obesity and not the inactivity that is responsible for the hypertension.

Alcohol consumption is still another life-style factor associated with an increased risk of hypertension. Studies have shown that people who regularly consume five ounces or more of alcohol a day have a higher incidence of hypertension than nondrinkers.

HIGH BLOOD PRESSURE IN THE ELDERLY

Hypertension among the elderly often poses special dilemmas. Some studies, such as one involving several thousand men undergoing treatment in

Veterans Administration hospitals, have found that cardiovascular mortality is lowered by treating high blood pressure among all age groups, including the elderly. But the approaches to treatment may be somewhat different. For example, many older people may have higher-than-normal systolic readings and normal or near-normal diastolic readings. This may be a result of the aging process, in which the blood vessels lose some of their elasticity. Some experts feel that there is little benefit in trying to lower this type of systolic hypertension, but more studies are needed before guidelines can be established.

As we grow older, the manner in which we metabolize drugs also may change. Therefore, dosages or the types of drugs used may be somewhat different for older hypertensive patients than for those who are younger.

3
Establishing the Diagnosis

Most people are shocked to learn that they have high blood pressure. Of the more than thirty-eight million Americans with hypertension, the American Heart Association estimates that about 30 percent do not know they have the disease. Typically, the disease may be present for fifteen or twenty years, or even longer, before it is diagnosed. By that time, it often has advanced to the point where irreversible damage has been done to the heart, kidneys, brain, or eyes. Many people find this hard to believe. How can a person have a potentially life-threatening disease and not even know it? This is why hypertension is called the "silent killer."

WARNING SIGNS

Characteristically, hypertension does not produce symptoms until it reaches an advanced stage. This means that a person can harbor the disease for fifteen or twenty years without ever feeling sick. When symptoms do occur, they tend to be vague and easily misinterpreted. Many people with hypertension never experience any of the symptoms described below; others will recall that they had experienced some warning signs, but either ignored them or attributed them to other causes.

Headaches are the most common symptom associated with high blood pressure, but there is no specific type of headache that indicates it is caused by hypertension. The pain may be mild and dull or intense and throbbing. It can occur anywhere in the head. It may be persistent or come-and-go. Of course, headaches have many causes, but any recurring headache is a sign to see a doctor.

Fatigue or unexplained tiredness is another possible symptom of hypertension. Again, this is a vague symptom that accompanies many illnesses, or it may be attributed to overwork, psychological problems, the weather, or any number of other factors. The tiredness of hypertension is often accompanied by feelings of irritability or nervousness. Many patients, after being diagnosed as having high blood pressure, recall that they have felt tired and out-of-sorts for weeks or even months, without actually feeling sick. Others describe a constellation of symptoms: vague headaches, fatigue, malaise, pains in the arms and legs.

Frequent, sometimes severe, nosebleeds are experienced by some people with high blood pressure. These nosebleeds may be harder than usual to stop and may even require seeing a doctor to have the nose packed.

Dizzy spells are still other symptoms associated with hypertension. Since this symptom is often associated with an ear or balance problem rather than a sign of high blood pressure, it is often misinterpreted. Any recurring episodes of dizziness or vertigo are a warning to see a doctor.

Shortness of breath, a feeling of heaviness, puffiness, and swelling of the lower legs also may be caused by serious hypertension. Such symptoms may indicate congestive heart failure, a consequence of the heart's inability to pump out as much blood as it should. Excess fluid builds up in the lungs and other parts of the body.

Blurred vision or other eye problems may be caused by hypertension. The high blood pressure causes ruptures of some of the tiny blood vessels in the eye. In fact, it is not unusual for hypertension to be initially spotted during an eye examination.

The presence of protein in the urine or other signs of kidney damage are still other possible signs of high blood pressure. In some instances, the kidney damage may be caused by the high blood pressure; in others, the situation may be reversed and it will be a kidney problem that is causing the hypertension. The latter is referred to as secondary hypertension and might be curable if the kidney disorder can be eliminated or effectively treated.

There also are symptoms that many people mistakenly associate with hypertension which, in reality, have little or nothing to do with the disease. Feelings of tension or anxiety are a common example. While some people with hypertension are tense and uptight, others are calm and even-tempered. Continual stress and an inability to cope with it may be related to hypertension, but not necessarily so.

Many people associate a red or flushed appearance of the face with hypertension. Again, some people with hypertension may have a red face, but this is unlikely to be caused by the disease.

ESTABLISHING A DIAGNOSIS

There are still large numbers of people who do not know they have high blood pressure, even though great strides have been made in the last decade to identify them and get them into effective treatment programs.

Screening for hypertension became a national health priority in the early

1970s. Before that, many doctors themselves were unaware of the fact that high blood pressure was so common or such a serious public health problem. Government organizations like the National High Blood Pressure Education Program, a national effort sponsored by the National Institutes of Health; volunteer agencies like the American Heart Association; and medical institutions such as the Cleveland Clinic joined forces. The goal was to make all people, including physicians, more aware of the seriousness of hypertension.

Community health fairs offering free blood pressure measurements were held throughout the country. All physicians were urged to make blood pressure measurement a part of every patient visit. Pharmacists, dentists, and other health professionals also were urged to do blood pressure measurements. Coin-operated blood pressure machines were installed in airports, shopping centers, and other public places. The message was persistent and clear: "Hypertension is a serious problem and it's important to know whether you have it." The effort has met with considerable success. Although there are still millions of unidentified hypertensives who should be under treatment, more Americans than ever before are being effectively treated, with measurable results. As noted earlier, fatal strokes have declined by 45 percent in the last fifteen years. Deaths from heart attacks and kidney failure also have dropped, due in large part to the increased and more effective treatment of hypertension.

The diagnosis of hypertension is not as simple as was once assumed. Many people still have the notion that a single above-normal reading automatically means hypertension. Cleveland Clinic physicians have long recognized that several blood pressure measurements at different times and in different positions and situations may be needed to establish a diagnosis. Dr. Robert Tarazi, Vice President of the Cleveland Clinic Research Foundation, explains why:

"A large number of people are hyperreactors with labile hypertension. We will see patients whose blood pressure may be 160/100 or even higher when it is measured by a doctor in a medical setting. But at home or in other settings, these patients will have absolutely normal blood pressures. Extra care should be taken in diagnosing hypertension in a person with no signs of organ damage and no family history or other risk factors. A person with labile hypertension should be monitored regularly, but very often there is no need to prescribe lifelong drug therapy for a person whose blood pressure is normal most of the time."

Dr. Tarazi also notes that most patients have a deep psychological reaction to a diagnosis of hypertension, an observation echoed by many of the patients we spoke to. "At first, I was scared to death," recalls Miss Youngman. "Because of my family history and the fact that my father died of a heart attack at fifty, I suspected the same thing might happen to me," Mr. Rhodes said, "but I didn't want to face the facts. My family doctor had said my pressure was on the high side, but nothing to worry about. I wanted to believe him more than the real experts." While these are normal responses, Dr. Tarazi notes that care must be taken to avoid subjecting healthy people to the worries and fears elicited by a diagnosis of hypertension if any doubt exists.

"There are also economic consequences," he stresses. "People with high blood pressure are often labeled as poor insurance risks or are passed over for a promotion or new job." In fact, this happened to Mr. Rhodes. "I was the leading candidate for a major promotion just before I underwent bypass surgery in 1973," he recalls. "But this was killed as soon as doubts about my health were raised." He notes with pride that in the twelve years since his operation, his high blood pressure has been well controlled and "today I can work circles around a lot of younger men." He also has been able to get an unrestricted life insurance policy—something that was denied him at a much younger age before he embarked on antihypertensive therapy.

Regular blood pressure measurements should begin early in life. A measurement should be included in routine pediatric examinations, and it's a good idea for parents to keep track of their children's blood pressure readings. Studies have found that children who are on the high-normal end of the scale are more likely to develop hypertension at an early age. Also, hypertension does occur during childhood. Sometimes this is due to a kidney disorder or other disease, but often it is primary hypertension. Adolescents often develop high blood pressure during their growth spurt. This frequently normalizes, but studies also have found that this group has a higher-than-normal incidence of hypertension.

To establish a diagnosis of hypertension at the Cleveland Clinic, blood pressure measurements are taken on two or more visits. The diastolic measurements are averaged, and if the figure is 90 or higher, the patient is presumed to have hypertension. The systolic measurements are also averaged; an average of 160 or more is categorized as systolic hypertension. (See Table 3.1 for classifications of blood pressure.)

In confirming a diagnosis of hypertension at the Cleveland Clinic, a number of factors in addition to the blood pressure measurements are taken into consideration. A careful history of the patient's health background is obtained. Particular attention is paid to questions such as:

Is there a history of hypertension, heart attacks, strokes, or other cardiovascular disorders in your family?
Have you ever had any problems with your heart? Kidneys? Eyes?
Have you ever been told that your blood pressure is high? When?

Do you have diabetes or have you ever been told you have diabetes?

What is your weight history? Have you ever been more than ten or fifteen pounds overweight? Have you been on diets in the past? How much weight did you lose?

What kinds of foods do you generally eat? Do you eat a lot of processed foods? Do you add extra salt to what you eat at the table?

Do you use alcohol? About how many drinks a day do you usually have?

Are you on any drugs or medications? Do you take thyroid pills, oral contraceptives, other hormones, cortisone or other steroids, tranquilizers or other mood-altering drugs. Do you use a bronchodilator to relax bronchial muscle? Sodium bicarbonate?

Have there been any major changes in your life lately (death in the family, marriage, divorce, move, new job, etc.)? Do you feel that you are under a lot of stress?

Do you smoke cigarettes? Drink a lot of coffee? Eat a lot of licorice?

Have there been any changes in your general mood or outlook on life lately?

Patients also are asked about any symptoms they might have had that may be linked to high blood pressure. Questions might include:

Have you had headaches more often than usual lately?

Do you get nosebleeds?

Do you sometimes feel dizzy or light-headed? Do you suffer from fainting spells or blackouts? Are you bothered by ringing in the ears?

Do you sometimes have shortness of breath? Do you have trouble breathing when you're lying down? Does sitting up or using extra pillows help?

Do you have any pain or feelings of heaviness or discomfort in your chest? Do you have trouble climbing stairs or walking uphill?

Do your legs swell? Do you have unexplained weight gains of several pounds in a day or two?

Women are asked about their menstrual history, any problems during pregnancy, and whether they are taking oral contraceptives.

After a careful medical history is obtained, patients are given a physical examination by a physician. The purpose of the examination is twofold: to look for signs of organ damage from the high blood pressure and also to determine whether the high blood pressure may be caused by some other disorder. Blood pressure will be measured two or more times during the examination, with the patient seated or lying down and also while standing.

Special attention is paid to organs that are the main targets of damage

TABLE 3.1. CLASSIFICATIONS OF BLOOD PRESSURE

Diastolic Blood Pressure (mm Hg)	Classification
Less than 85	Normal
85 to 89	High Normal
90 to 104	Mild Hypertension
105 to 114	Moderate Hypertension
115 or higher	Severe Hypertension

Systolic Blood Pressure (mm Hg) (with diastolic readings of 90 or less)	Classification
140 or less	Normal
140 to 159	Borderline Isolated Systolic Hypertension
160 or higher	Isolated Systolic Hypertension

Note: A classification of borderline isolated systolic hypertension (140 to 159 mm Hg) or isolated systolic hypertension (160 or higher) takes precedence over a classification of high normal blood pressure (diastolic readings of 85 to 89) when both occur in the same person. A classification of high normal blood pressure (diastolic readings of 85 to 89) takes precedence over a classification of normal systolic pressure (140 or less) when both occur in the same person.

Adapted from The 1984 Report of the Joint National Committee on Detection, Evaluation, and Treatment of High Blood Pressure, U.S. Department of Health and Human Services, NIH Publication No. 84-1088, September 1984.

from high blood pressure. The eyes are examined carefully because they are a major target of hypertension and are also the only part of the body where a doctor can directly view the blood vessels. In particular, the doctor will look for any signs of swelling or edema of the optic disk (papilledema), hemorrhages of the tiny blood vessels in the eye, a narrowing or compression of the blood vessels in the eye, or other abnormalities that may be caused by high blood pressure.

Since the heart is another major target of hypertension, special attention is paid to it during the physical examination. The physician listens for any abnormal heart sounds or arrhythmias, murmurs, and increased heart rate. Heart size is also important; an enlarged heart is a common consequence of hypertension. A doctor can determine the size of the heart by tapping on the chest and listening to the sounds produced. Or a more precise measurement can be obtained by ultrasound examination or X ray. An electrocardiogram also tells a good deal about the heart's condition, and an exercise test with

TABLE 3.2. RECOMMENDED FOLLOWUP AFTER INITIAL MEASUREMENT FOR PEOPLE OVER 18

Diastolic Blood Pressure	Recommended Followup
85 or less	Recheck within 2 years.
85 to 90	Recheck within 1 year.
90 to 104	Recheck promptly (within 2 months) to confirm diagnosis of hypertension.
105 to 114	Evaluate or refer promptly (within 2 weeks) to source of care.
115 or higher	Evaluate or refer immediately to source of care.

Systolic Blood Pressure (when diastolic reading is 90 or less)	Recommended Followup
140 or less	Recheck within 2 years.
140 to 199	Recheck promptly (within 2 months) to confirm diagnosis.
200 or higher	Evaluate or refer promptly (within 2 weeks) to source of care.

Note: If recommendations for followup of diastolic and systolic blood pressures are different, the shorter recommended time period supersedes and a referral for care supersedes recommendation for a recheck.

Adapted from The 1984 Report of the Joint National Committee on Detection, Evaluation, and Treatment of High Blood Pressure, U.S. Department of Health and Human Services, NIH Publication No. 84-1088, September 1984.

EKG monitoring also may be performed to determine the heart's work capacity.

The doctor listens for any abnormal sounds in the carotid artery, the blood vessel that runs along the neck and supplies blood to the brain. The neck also will be examined for any distended veins and the thyroid, which rests under the Adam's apple in the front of the neck, will be felt for any signs of enlargement. The abdomen is examined for signs of enlarged kidneys, aneurysm (ballooning out) of the aorta, and any abnormal sounds in the blood vessels. The legs and feet are examined for signs of edema and circulatory problems, such as diminished or absent pulses.

Laboratory tests include a complete blood count; a blood analysis for cholesterol and triglyceride levels; measurements of blood glucose (sugar) and serum potassium, uric acid and creatinine; a urinalysis; and other tests that may be indicated by findings in the physical examination or patient history.

During this physical examination, the doctor also will look for signs that the hypertension may be secondary to some other disorder. For example, abdominal masses or murmurs may indicate kidney disease; delayed or absent pulses in the femoral artery are a sign of coarctation (narrowing or stricture) of the aorta. Cushing's syndrome, a disease caused by excessive production of adrenal hormones, may cause high blood pressure. Pheochromocytoma, a tumor that secretes stress hormones such as epinephrine and norepinephrine, also causes high blood pressure. Because they are so rare, elaborate testing for the presence of these diseases is not done unless there are suspicious signs or unless antihypertensive treatment does not produce the expected lowering in blood pressure.

Patients may be taught how to measure their own blood pressure at home (see p. 148) to see how it compares with the readings obtained in a doctor's office. This may be particularly important if there are no signs of organ damage and the diastolic pressures obtained in the doctor's office vary widely or are in a borderline category.

Once hypertension is diagnosed, the next step is to determine its severity and to plan a treatment program. (See Table 3.2 for recommended follow-up.) The entire diagnostic process may take a couple of months and will require two or more physician visits. But it is worth the time and effort to learn as much as possible about the type of hypertension involved because this will lead to a more precise and effective treatment program.

4
Nondrug Treatments of Hypertension

A diagnosis of hypertension usually means lifelong treatment. Most people assume that this means taking one or more drugs each day for the rest of their lives, a prospect that no one relishes. But, as stressed repeatedly throughout this book, the risk of not treating may mean a life shortened by heart disease, stroke, or kidney failure, as well as the very real prospect of blindness and increasing disability. In short, considering the alternative, taking one or more pills per day is not so bad.

Even so, there are a substantial number of people with borderline or mild hypertension whose blood pressure can be controlled by nondrug treatments. As explained by Dr. Gifford: "It is always desirable to avoid taking drugs if the same goals can be accomplished by other means." In starting treatment for mild hypertension, Dr. Gifford and his Cleveland Clinic colleagues begin with a three- to six-month trial of nondrug treatment. If, after that time, the diastolic blood pressure has not fallen to 90 or less, then antihypertensive drugs will be prescribed.

Although nondrug treatment of mild hypertension may be preferable to taking drugs, it often means making life-style changes that are more difficult for many people to follow than taking one or two pills a day. "Too often both the doctor and patient are willing to settle for a lesser degree of blood pressure control rather than sticking to the necessary life-style changes," Dr. Gifford notes. "It's the patient who is hurt most when ineffective nondrug therapy is used as an excuse to delay the prescribing of a more effective drug treatment."

Having voiced these warnings, Dr. Gifford and his colleagues work very hard to help Clinic patients lower their blood pressures through nondrug means. These are briefly summarized here and discussed in more detail in the following chapters.

WEIGHT LOSS

Since up to 60 percent of all hypertensive patients are obese, losing excess weight becomes a number one priority. A number of studies have shown that a weight loss of ten or more pounds will reduce blood pressure for many people with mild hypertension who are overweight. In general, the greater the weight loss the greater the drop in blood pressure. "Often, normal blood pressure is achieved by patients with mild hypertension who lose more than twenty pounds," Dr. Gifford says. "Weight control for the obese hypertensive patient is probably more effective than restricting salt in lowering blood pressure. Unfortunately, weight control is difficult to achieve and maintain." Most people who manage to lose weight gain it back within two years. This weight gain is usually accompanied by a rise in blood pressure to its former level.

LOWERING SALT CONSUMPTION

Excessive sodium consumption has long been linked to hypertension, and there is little doubt among experts that sodium in some way can cause high blood pressure in people with a genetic predisposition. How sodium actually causes high blood pressure is unknown; it has been shown, however, that hypertension can be lowered somewhat by limiting sodium consumption to two grams a day. This is the amount of sodium in five grams of table salt. (Five grams is about one teaspoonful.)

At first, this seems like it should be easy to accomplish. After all, a teaspoonful sounds like a lot of salt—certainly more than was provided on the bland, boring rice diet once used to treat high blood pressure. Most people don't realize that the average American consumes many times that much salt —ten to twenty grams or two to four teaspoons—and that salt is added to almost all prepared foods.

"People have to know where to look for the salt," stresses Linda Nichols, a registered dietitian assigned to the Cleveland Clinic hypertension division. "It often takes a lot of education and counseling with both the patient and food preparer to develop a diet that is appetizing, especially if the patient is accustomed to eating a lot of salt."

Because so many people consume a large number of meals away from home, the Cleveland Clinic dietitians also include instruction in eating out as part of their low-salt education program. "People are increasingly salt conscious," Ms. Nichols says. "Many restaurants feature low-salt selections and people can always ask to have their dishes prepared with other flavorings."

Even so, salt restriction can be difficult and many patients who think they are eating virtually no salt are, in reality, consuming too much. If excessive sodium intake is suspected as a cause for continued high blood pressure, Clinic doctors will ask a patient to collect all urine voided over a twenty-four-hour period. "This will give an objective estimate of how much sodium is being consumed," Dr. Gifford explains. "The objective is not to chastise the patient; instead, our intent is to determine whether a low-sodium diet is going to be effective in controlling blood pressure. If the test shows that there has been a high-salt intake, even though the patient feels that he has adhered to a low-salt diet, we may be able to review the eating record and find unsuspected sources of sodium, such as processed foods. Many people feel that if they don't add salt to foods they are following a low-salt diet. This simply is not true—most salt is 'hidden' in processed foods, many of which don't taste at all salty." (See chapter 6.)

EXERCISE

Studies have shown that cardiovascular exercise conditioning, involving such activities as brisk walking, jogging, cycling, swimming, or other aerobic exercises, can produce a modest lowering of blood pressure in patients with mild hypertension. "The data for exercise as a nondrug treatment of hypertension are less convincing than for low-sodium and low-calorie diets," Dr. Gifford observes. Nevertheless, he adds, "Judicious exercise should be an integral part of a nondrug regimen for hypertension." (See chapter 7.) Isometric exercises, such as weight lifting, push-ups, and Nautilus workouts, should be avoided because these raise blood pressure and do not provide the cardiovascular conditioning of isotonic, or aerobic, exercise.

BEHAVIOR MODIFICATION

A number of behavior modification techniques—yoga, biofeedback, relaxation response, transcendental meditation, stress management—have been advocated as nondrug treatments for hypertension. "These techniques may be useful in helping a person cope with stress, but their long-term value in treating hypertension has not been demonstrated," Dr. Gifford says. Any lowering in blood pressure is usually short-term, and not reliable enough to be advocated as an effective treatment. These behavior modification techniques should not be confused with life-style modification or changes, which include weight control, exercise, and stopping smoking.

STOPPING SMOKING

Although smoking a cigarette produces an almost immediate rise in blood pressure, this tends to be temporary. There is speculation that heavy smoking may produce a sustained rise in blood pressure, but this has not been proved. "Nevertheless," Dr. Gifford notes, "cigarette smoking is a potent, independent risk factor for coronary disease and sudden death and it should be emphatically discouraged." (For guidelines on stopping smoking, see chapter 8.)

ALCOHOL CONSUMPTION

Consumption of more than two or three ounces of alcohol a day increases blood pressure. "It has been suggested that excessive alcohol intake may be the most common form of potentially curable hypertension in the United States," Dr. Gifford says, adding: "Any nondrug approach to lowering blood pressure should include moderation of alcohol."

Alcoholic drinks are also a source of calories; cutting back on beer, wine, or spirits not only lowers alcohol consumption but also eliminates extra calories from the diet.

DIETARY SUPPLEMENTS

There have been preliminary reports suggesting that supplements of calcium, potassium, or magnesium may lower high blood pressure. "There may be some theoretic validity to these claims," Dr. Gifford notes, "but so far there have been no good clinical studies to back them up." Cleveland Clinic physicians may prescribe a potassium supplement for patients whose potassium levels are low because of antihypertensive drugs, but mineral supplements are not routinely included as part of the treatment of the disease itself.

THE VALUE OF NONDRUG APPROACHES IN COMBINATION WITH DRUG THERAPY

Unless there are individual reasons for not trying nondrug approaches in the initial treatment of mild hypertension, Cleveland Clinic physicians prescribe some or all of the measures described above for three to six months before starting antihypertensive medications. "We can usually tell in that time whether the patient is going to get the needed results from a nondrug regimen," Dr. Donald Vidt says. But even if drugs are needed, there is still value to be gained from the nondrug measures.

Cleveland Clinic doctors have found that patients who lose weight, cut back on salt and alcohol, stop smoking, and start exercising usually can get by on much lower doses of antihypertensive drugs than those who don't modify their life-styles. This reduces the risk of side effects and also lowers the cost of treatment. Perhaps even more important, these patients tend to feel better.

Mrs. Olds, one of the Clinic patients described in chapter 2, is a good example. About a year ago, she and her husband joined a health club and she took up swimming. Circulatory problems in her legs make it difficult for her to walk or do other aerobic exercises, but she can swim for an hour a day without difficulty. "I stop and rest now and then, and I don't break any speed records," she says with characteristic good humor. "The fact is, I can't remember when I have felt this good! I'm positive it's because of the exercise. Before, I didn't realize how sedentary I was because I was always busy. But I wasn't getting any real physical activity. Swimming has made all the difference."

In addition to undertaking a regular exercise program, Mrs. Olds has lost more than thirty pounds since undergoing coronary bypass surgery and has been able to maintain her reduced weight for the first time since she was a student. She also watches her salt intake. Although Mrs. Olds still takes four different antihypertensive drugs a day plus insulin for her diabetes, her present regimen is a far cry from the thirty pills a day she needed a few years ago.

5
The Importance of Weight Control

It is hard to overemphasize the importance of weight control in treating hypertension. Overweight people of all ages are more likely to develop high blood pressure than are people of normal weight. Although the mechanism by which excess weight produces high blood pressure is unknown, statistics abound pointing to obesity as an important risk factor for developing hypertension. (Obesity also increases the risk of a heart attack, adult diabetes, and certain types of cancer.) As noted earlier, studies have found that up to 60 percent of all hypertensives are obese, defined as being at least 20 percent above normal weight. (See Table 5.1, "Desirable Weights for Men and Women.")

The National Health Examination Survey on blood pressure among the young found that weight was the most important predictor of whether a child or adolescent would have high blood pressure. Epidemiologic studies from around the world have shown that in most populations an increase in weight is accompanied by a rise in blood pressure. In the United States, a rise in blood pressure has been correlated with increasing age, but epidemiologists note that this occurs only in countries where weight also increases with age. In population groups where older people remain thin, there is no increase in blood pressure with age; indeed, in some societies, blood pressure actually declines slightly as the people grow older.

There are a number of explanations of how increased weight may raise blood pressure. Obviously, added weight puts an extra burden on the circulatory system, causing the heart to work harder to supply enough blood to the extra tissue. Recent studies have also linked abnormal insulin secretion in overweight people with increased sodium and fluid retention and a rise in blood pressure. Other unidentified factors also may play a role; not everyone who is overweight develops hypertension and not all people with hypertension are overweight. Still, doctors who treat high blood pressure agree that weight control is a major priority, both in treating hypertension and in preventing its development.

Unfortunately, losing weight and maintaining that reduction is very diffi-

TABLE 5.1. DESIRABLE WEIGHTS FOR MEN AND WOMEN

According to Height and Frame. Ages 25 and Over

Height (in shoes)	WEIGHT IN POUNDS (IN INDOOR CLOTHING)		
	Small Frame	Medium Frame	Large Frame
MEN			
5'2"	112–120	118–129	126–141
5'3"	115–123	121–133	129–144
5'4"	118–126	124–136	132–148
5'5"	121–129	127–139	135–152
5'6"	124–133	130–143	138–156
5'7"	128–137	134–147	142–161
5'8"	132–141	138–152	147–166
5'9"	136–145	142–156	151–170
5'10"	140–150	146–160	155–174
5'11"	144–154	150–165	159–179
6'0"	148–158	154–170	164–184
6'1"	152–162	158–175	168–189
6'2"	156–167	162–180	173–194
6'3"	160–171	167–185	178–199
6'4"	164–175	172–190	182–204
WOMEN			
4'10"	92–98	96–107	104–119
4'11"	94–101	98–110	106–122
5'0"	96–104	101–113	109–125
5'1"	99–107	104–116	112–128
5'2"	102–110	107–119	115–131
5'3"	105–113	110–122	118–134
5'4"	108–116	113–126	121–138
5'5"	111–119	116–130	125–142
5'6"	114–123	120–135	129–146
5'7"	118–127	124–139	133–150
5'8"	122–131	128–143	137–154
5'9"	126–135	132–147	141–158
5'10"	130–140	136–151	145–163
5'11"	134–144	140–155	149–168
6'0"	138–148	144–159	153–173

cult for most people. There is much that we do not know about obesity: Why do some people become fat and others stay slim? Overeating is one obvious reason, but it is not the whole story.

Studies by the National Center for Health Statistics have found that, despite our national preoccupation with dieting and weight, Americans weigh more now than at any time in the past. The average adult male is now twenty-five to thirty pounds overweight and the average American woman weighs fifteen to thirty pounds more than what is considered desirable. Even these figures may be misleading because they are based on weight tables that many experts feel are higher than they should be. At the same time, studies show that the average American today actually eats less than his or her counterpart at the turn of the century. Why, if people actually are eating less, is widespread obesity such a problem? The answer lies in our labor-saving life-style, lack of exercise, and in the composition of our diets.

There is no doubt that Americans today enjoy an abundance and variety of food unprecedented in human history. Modern agriculture and transportation make it possible for us to enjoy low-cost foods from every corner of the world. Our food prices are lower than any other country, and despite reports of hunger in America, in general, we consume a greater variety and more food than any other society in history.

The way we eat also is undergoing change. At one time, most meals were consumed with the entire family gathered around a table at home. Today, very few families manage even one traditional daily meal together. We skip breakfast or eat it on the run, eat lunch at school, the office, or in a restaurant, and perhaps manage to have dinner together a few times a week. Fast food, which tends to be high in saturated fat, calories, and salt, has become part of the American way of life. In the typical American diet, about 40 percent of the calories consumed come from fats, with 15 to 17 percent being animal or other saturated fats. About 20 percent of our calories come from protein, mostly meats, and the remaining 40 percent are from carbohydrates, with sugar accounting for more than half of that amount. At the turn of the century, the typical diet was much lower in animal fat, protein, and sugar and much higher in complex carbohydrates (breads, cereals, vegetables, and fruits) and fiber or roughage. Our high-fat, low-fiber diet is a major cause of the widespread elevated blood cholesterol among Americans—a major risk factor for an early heart attack. If a person with high blood cholesterol also has high blood pressure—and millions of Americans have this unfortunate combination—the risk more than doubles.

In addition to changes in the makeup of our diet and the way we eat, our changed life-style also accounts for the preponderance of obesity among Americans. Our bodies are designed to burn up the food we consume. A certain number of calories are needed to carry on basic metabolic processes; even when we sleep or are otherwise inactive, the body requires fuel for circulation, tissue repair, and other mostly involuntary functions. The rest of what we consume is meant to be expended in physical activity. Obviously, not all activities require the same levels of energy (caloric) expenditure. Sitting watching TV or reading a book or the newspaper requires a minimal expenditure of calories, walking at a leisurely pace requires more, and heavy physical labor or vigorous exercise burns up even more. The calories that we don't burn up are converted to body fat and stored for future use. The problem is, because so many of us lead essentially sedentary lives, we tend to keep on storing calories until we have a marked weight problem.

Even with today's emphasis on fitness and the popularity of jogging and other physical activities, studies show that only a third or less of all American adults exercise on a regular basis. In reality, most of us lead very sedentary lives compared to our forefathers. We use a car to travel even a few blocks; our houses are filled with labor-saving devices, and even jobs that are considered "hard labor" are likely to involve more use of machines than human muscle. So we may eat less than Americans a century ago, but we still consume more calories than we need, resulting in more than 150 million overweight Americans.

The Framingham study has found that overweight people have an increased mortality rate from a number of causes: heart attacks, certain cancers, and diabetes are leading examples of obesity-related diseases. Clearly, our "good life" and abundance of food is contrary to good health and a long life. And it is understandable that nutrition counseling is a major focus of patient education at the Cleveland Clinic.

Dr. Helen Brown, a Cleveland Clinic pioneer in the dietary aspects of hypertension and coronary disease, emphasizes that the eating pattern now recommended for most hypertensive patients "is basically a rather simple, nutritious diet that is ideal for everyone. Over the years, we have moved away from the rigid, highly restrictive diets that were once recommended for our patients to an approach that is based on the principles of total good nutrition —reduced intake of fats, total calories, and salt, and more emphasis on fruits, vegetables, and a variety of foods to provide the needed vitamins and minerals." Today's simplified eating patterns are grounded largely in prudence and common sense, and are embodied in the new American Heart Association dietary recommendations.

In introducing its new dietary goals last year, the AHA noted: "Over the past ten years, there has been a shift in thinking regarding the design of dietary treatment patterns. A unified rather than a categorical approach is now emphasized." In the past, an antihypertension diet may have concentrated mostly on salt reduction. Today, the emphasis is on a total approach: a reduction in salt and saturated fats, caloric consumption to meet individual needs, and a diet that provides a better balance of complex carbohydrates, protein, and fats.

Cleveland Clinic dietitians also recognize that any dietary change is hard for most people to accomplish. Food is an important part of life; most people do and should enjoy eating. For a diet to be successful, it must take into account a person's food preferences, attitudes toward eating, and social demands. Most diets fail because they restrict caloric intake, usually by prescribing a rigid eating pattern. The diet may accomplish the weight loss, but it does not tackle the basic underlying problem, namely, ingrained faulty eating habits. Typically, a dieter really wants to lose weight and will make considerable efforts to follow the prescribed regimen, often feeling hungry and deprived a good deal of the time, until a certain amount of weight is lost. And then he or she celebrates the dieting success with a big meal, perhaps even a binge on favorite foods that have been denied while on the diet. Before long, the pounds that have been shed with so much difficulty are regained, very often with a few extra. The person ends up feeling guilty and out of control —another dieting failure.

Like other aspects of treating hypertension (as well as obesity, high cholesterol, and other diet-related problems), eating patterns must be altered for life. But this does not mean that a person has to *diet* for life. Instead, it means that the person must learn a healthy way of eating—one that provides the right number of calories, balance of nutrients, and enjoyment. For people who have been on and off crash diets, often for years, this may sound impossible. The fact is, it is easier than "dieting," which is usually doomed from the outset because most diets require that a person try to deny one of our strongest drives—hunger. The trick is to learn how to put hunger to work for you instead of trying the impossible, that is, overcoming or denying hunger.

Of course, satisfying hunger is not the only reason people eat. We eat for enjoyment, to overcome frustration, to be sociable, to counter boredom. Before eating patterns can be changed, a person must know and understand them. This means keeping a careful food diary. In counseling patients with hypertension (or any other diet-related disorder), dietitians invariably start by asking patients to keep a careful record of all food that is consumed over a period of time. Dr. Brown says that jotting down all that is eaten on a typical day is usually sufficient, although some dietitians may ask that patients keep a food diary for a week or more. Also, some patients find that simply writing down what they eat is an aid in spotting faulty eating patterns and a useful tool in adopting healthier food habits.

When keeping a food diary, you should record what is eaten as soon as

possible; sitting down at the end of the day and trying to remember everything that was consumed since morning is a difficult, if not impossible, task.
"Most people remember the meat or main dish," Dr. Brown explains, "but
forget that they had a vegetable with cream sauce, salad with blue cheese
dressing, a cocktail or two, a handful of peanuts, and so forth."

TABLE 5.2. SAMPLE FOOD RECORD

Date _____

Check Type of Day:

_____ Workday

_____ Non-Workday

Where Food Is Eaten				
At Home	Away	TIME	FOOD EATEN	AMOUNT

You can use the form in Table 5.2 or simply jot down what you eat in a
pocket notebook or some other convenient record book. Don't forget the
drinks; many are major sources of calories. Be sure to record the time the
food and drink were consumed, along with the circumstances: a regular meal,
midmorning snack, after work with friends, a snack consumed while watch-

ing TV, etc. Many people eat almost unconsciously while performing other tasks; making a conscious effort to note this type of munching and recording it in a diary can be valuable in changing.

With a food diary in hand, a dietitian can analyze it and show patients areas in which modification can make a big difference. Everyone has individual food preferences and eating habits that are built over a lifetime. Most of us include the basics of good nutrition among the foods we happen to like, but most of us also harbor misconceptions about food. Recognizing and changing these may require expert help. Many people make the mistake of trying to change everything all at once. Dietitians recommend identifying the major problem areas and tackling them first. For example, if overweight is the big problem, a modified eating program should concentrate first on losing the excess weight rather than overloading the patient with other life-style changes. Once the weight is under control, then other problem areas can be tackled. Often problem areas are closely related, and in solving one, others naturally fall into place. For example, cutting back on fats is the number one priority in both reducing weight and lowering high cholesterol. Therefore, the dietary changes that lower cholesterol will also reduce calories—a gram of fat contains 9 calories compared to 4 calories per gram in carbohydrates and protein. By substituting foods high in complex carbohydrates for red meat and other high-fat foods, total calories will be reduced.

THE MEANING OF HUNGER

Increasingly, dietitians and nutritionists are recognizing that most diet failures can be traced to a misinterpretation of the role of hunger. Appetite and hunger are controlled by the brain. Blood sugar (glucose) is the body's major fuel. Almost all of the carbohydrate and part of the protein we consume are converted to blood glucose to be used as fuel. When blood sugar levels fall, the body goes into action to replenish it. As glucose stores from the liver are mobilized, the appetite center in the brain sends out hunger signals. Typically, people on a diet will try to deny or suppress these hunger signals. As ready stores of glucose are consumed, the hunger signals become stronger. The body does not recognize the difference between voluntary abstaining from food and starving, as in a concentration camp or during a famine. Metabolic processes slow down in an effort to conserve food, and body stores of fat and lean tissue are mobilized to provide the fuel the body needs to keep going, even with its metabolic thermostat set at a lower level.

Eventually the feelings of hunger become too strong to keep denying, and the dieter quickly eats something—typically a sweet which provides a quick rise in blood sugar. Hunger is appeased, but only temporarily. The surge in blood sugar is quickly used up, and the cycle begins again, sending out even stronger hunger signals. This is what might happen in a dieter's typical day:

Most of us don't wake up ravishingly hungry, even though blood sugar may be low from a twelve-hour fast. Skipping breakfast or getting by with a cup of coffee and glass of juice is relatively easy and a common pattern. By midmorning, true feelings of hunger set in. The dieter may be able to ignore them or temporarily satisfy them with a cup of coffee, cigarette, and perhaps a candy bar or doughnut. By the time lunch rolls around, the dieter is "starving," but determined to be strong, and again either skips the meal or makes do with a minimal amount of food. By dinnertime, the hunger can no longer be denied and the dieter ends up consuming everything in sight. In that one meal, he or she may consume 2,500 or more calories—twice the entire day's allotment—and still feel so hungry that several trips to the refrigerator are made before finally going to bed. Sometimes, the person mistakenly thinks that because so little food was consumed during the day, a big dinner won't matter. More often, the dieter feels guilty and out-of-control, determined to do better the next day, only to have the pattern repeat itself. Even people who manage to stick to a diet will end up overeating when they have reached their weight goal simply because they have not learned how to put hunger to work for them.

One trick to managing hunger is to satisfy it with a small amount of food at the first signals. This may mean eating several small, well-timed meals during the course of the day. Most of us have been taught that we should have three square meals a day, and that snacking in between is to be avoided, and many people manage very well by eating three well-balanced meals a day. But others may become so hungry that they end up overeating at dinner. A couple of high-fiber crackers or a snack of raw vegetables will prevent this. Of course, constant eating will add pounds, as will snacking on candy, chips, and other high-calorie foods, but learning how to time eating to avoid overpowering hunger is an important key to long-term weight control.

For more specific guidelines, see the Cleveland Clinic's "Simplified Weight Control Diet" at the end of this chapter.

EATING FOR OTHER REASONS

Of course, hunger is not the only motivation for eating. All of us eat for many other reasons. People who keep food diaries are often surprised to learn some of the reasons that prompt them to eat. Some people eat simply because someone urges them to, perhaps harking back to childhood and an anxious mother who constantly worried that her child was not getting enough to eat. Others eat to ease tension or feelings of anxiety, or simply because the food is there. Food is often perceived as a substitute for a goal that is less attainable or as something of a security blanket.

Studies have shown that there may be an inborn tendency to eat in response to external stimuli. Dr. Robert Milstein, a researcher at Yale University and an expert in obesity, found that newborn infants whose parents are obese are more likely to respond to sweet tastes than babies with normal-weight parents. This may explain why obesity seems to "run in families." Still, cues other than hunger that prompt us to eat can be recognized and dealt with in more constructive ways. True hunger is the body's way of protecting us from starvation; a person whose food intake is controlled by hunger alone can learn to recognize hunger and eat until the hunger is satisfied. Eating in response to other stimuli or motivations may be more difficult to sort out, but it's not impossible. If a person invariably finds that he or she heads for the refrigerator after an argument with a spouse, for example, help may be needed finding other ways of responding to the emotional conflict. Eating out of boredom may be overcome by exercise or finding some interest other than food.

THE ROLE OF CALORIES

Although obesity is a complex problem with many causes, some of which are not fully understood, one central fact stands out: In most cases, excessive weight comes from consuming excessive calories. For example, if you consume 100 calories more per day than you use up, you will gain a pound (3,500 calories) in about five weeks. Similarly, if you burn up 100 calories more than you consume per day, you will lose a pound in five weeks. Of course, if you need to lose thirty or forty pounds, it will take many months to shed the unwanted weight at that rate. The process can be speeded up by consuming fewer calories and, at the same time, increasing physical activity to burn up even more calories.

Any sensible weight-loss program calls for a reduction in total calories consumed coupled with a concerted effort to modify eating habits for lifelong control. There are definite hazards to going on and off diets. The seesaw effect of weight loss followed by weight gain followed by another attempt at weight loss puts extra strain on the cardiovascular system. Blood pressure goes up and down with the weight cycles. During fasting or extreme reductions of food consumption, the body will begin to metabolize its own lean tissue for fuel. This can cause cardiac arrhythmia and sudden death. What's more, each crash diet alters the body's metabolic rate. When deprived of food, the body attempts to protect itself from starvation by lowering its basal metabolism—the number of calories needed to maintain vital functions. The metabolic thermostat is reset, so to speak, at a lower rate. This is why people find they put on more pounds with less food after a crash diet.

After analyzing food habits and determining eating habits that need modification, the next step toward successful weight control involves reducing the total intake of food to provide for a loss of one to two pounds a week.

"In the past, patients were often told they had to learn how to count calories in order to lose weight," Dr. Brown notes. "While weight-reduction obviously involves lowering your total intake of calories, this can be accomplished without a complicated regimen of weighing or measuring food and consulting calorie tables." For example, Dr. Brown suggests, "You can eliminate four hundred calories a day from the average diet by buying lean cuts of meat and trimming off all visible fat, and cutting down on the amount of margarine or oils used as spreads, salad dressing, or in cooking." Avoiding fast foods, sweets, and high-calorie snacks is also a relatively easy way to reduce total food consumption.

The food lists and meal plan outlined in the "Simplified Weight Control Diet" provide the basic guidelines for adopting a healthy eating pattern that is suitable for the entire family. A person who is markedly overweight and relatively inactive will need to restrict food intake more than people who are moderately active. A dietitian or other health professional trained in nutrition counseling can offer specific guidelines in developing a diet to meet individual needs. Care should be taken, however, to make sure that the person is indeed qualified to give sound nutrition advice. As noted by Connie Sersig of the Cleveland Clinic Patient Education Department, "Nutrition counseling is one area in which there is a tremendous amount of quackery or well-meaning but unqualified practitioners." Unfortunately, there are no uniform standards for nutritionists—virtually anyone can set up practice as a nutrition counselor. At the very least, the person should be a registered dietitian and preferably have experience in working with people with cardiovascular problems. A physician or a hospital dietetics department usually can provide names of qualified dietitians who can work with hypertensive patients to develop a satisfactory diet/eating program.

CREATIVE SUBSTITUTIONS

Most people have the notion that self-denial is an essential part of dieting, and this is another common reason for diet failure. Mrs. Blake, one of the Cleveland Clinic patients described in chapter 2, talks about her "fatal weakness for ice cream." "I simply can't walk by an ice cream parlor if I have any money in my purse," she says. "If it's in the refrigerator, I'll eat it." Mrs.

Blake confesses that she feels guilty each time she succumbs; she knows that she needs to lose weight and she has tried many times in the past. But eventually filling up on high-calorie foods like ice cream wins out and her weight goes back up.

Instead of trying to fight a losing battle with a favorite food, nutrition counselors advise that it is easier to find an acceptable substitute for that food —one that satisfies our basic liking for certain foods but will still fit in with our dietary goals. In the case of something like ice cream, which is high in calories and saturated fats, a person might try low-fat ice milk, which tastes a lot like ice cream but has fewer calories and fat, or some of the newer frozen tofu creations that also taste like ice cream but are low in saturated fats, or frozen fruit ices, some of which are sugar-free, low in calories, and have no fat. They may not be as rich as ice cream, but many people find them a highly acceptable substitute that they can enjoy without feeling guilty or out of control.

Beverages represent another area where creative substitution can save calories which most people are not aware of. "When I realized how many calories are in soft drinks, I tried some of the noncalorie ones. I didn't like the taste, so I switched to fruit juice," one Cleveland Clinic patient said. Unfortunately, fruit juices contain as many or more calories than many soft drinks. An eight-ounce cup of fresh orange juice, for example, has about 110 calories, a cup of grapefruit juice has about 100 calories, and a cup of canned apple juice has about 120 calories. Eight ounces of Pepsi or Coke have around 104 calories; eight ounces of 7-Up or ginger ale each have about 96. Of course, fruit juices also contain important vitamins and minerals that are not found in soft drinks, but if four or five cups of fruit juice are consumed each day— not an unusual amount for someone who drinks juice instead of water when thirsty—up to 550 extra calories may unwittingly be consumed.

Water, of course, has no calories, it costs little or nothing, and satisfies thirst. Still, many people don't like water. Seltzer, carbonated water, may be an acceptable substitute that contains neither calories nor salt. Some of the new fruit-flavored seltzers are a good substitute for sugar-free soft drinks; they are less expensive and don't have an unpleasant aftertaste. Or a squeeze of lemon can be added to plain seltzer. Keeping a pitcher of ice water with slices of lemon or oranges in it in the refrigerator is another possible substitute that is refreshing and calorie-free. Very weak iced tea with lemon is still another possibility.

REDUCING FATS

As noted earlier, 40 percent of calories in the average American diet are from fats, and a large percentage of these are from animal or other saturated fats. This high-fat diet is responsible for the fact that so many Americans have dangerously high levels of cholesterol. Reducing high cholesterol is particularly important for patients with high blood pressure because the presence of both compounds the risk of a heart attack. In recent years, Americans have become more cholesterol-conscious. The American Heart Association estimates that the average American now consumes about 450 to 500 milligrams of cholesterol a day, considerably less than a decade ago. The decline is attributed to reduced consumption of red meat, butter, and eggs—all major sources of saturated fats. But we still have a way to go to achieve the Heart Association's recommended average daily consumption of 300 milligrams of cholesterol.

Although Americans are much more cholesterol-conscious today, there are still many misconceptions about fats and cholesterol and their role in the development of heart disease. A certain amount of fat must be consumed in the diet to provide essential fatty acids, which the body requires for a number of functions. Essential fatty acids are found mostly in polyunsaturated fatty acids, such as corn oil, safflower, soybean, and certain other vegetable oils. At least one tablespoon of a polyunsaturated oil is needed each day to provide enough essential fatty acids. In contrast, saturated fatty acids are not needed in the diet at all; the body can manufacture all that it needs. Saturated fats come mostly from animal sources—fatty meats, butter, whole milk, cheese, etc. There also are vegetable sources of saturated fats; coconut or palm oils, vegetable shortening, and hardened or hydrogenated oils are examples. Saturated fats tend to be hard at room temperature and, when consumed in the diet, they raise blood cholesterol. Commercially baked goods and fast foods tend to be very high in saturated fats.

Unsaturated fats are liquid or soft and come from vegetable sources, and they lower blood cholesterol. Monosaturated fats fall between saturated and unsaturated fats; they include olive and peanut oil and the oils found in avocados and cashews. These fats also lower cholesterol, but not as much as polyunsaturated oil.

Contrary to popular belief, cholesterol is not a fat but a sterol lipid, a waxy, fat-like alcohol of high molecular weight. It is found only in animal products. Egg yolks, organ meats, animal fats, cream, and cheese are major sources. Cholesterol is essential for a number of vital body processes, including nerve function, reproduction, and maintenance of cell structures, but it is not necessary to consume any cholesterol in the diet; the body can manufacture all that it needs.

Several types of cholesterol circulate through the body. Since cholesterol is a lipid, a fat-like substance, it is not soluble in water, the major component of the blood. In order for a lipid molecule to circulate through the blood, it must be attached to a water-soluble substance; namely, a protein molecule. When the lipid and protein molecules are combined, they form a molecule called a lipoprotein.

Lipoproteins of different sizes and weights, or densities, circulate through the body. The smallest and heaviest are the high-density lipoproteins, or HDL. HDL cholesterol has the largest proportion of protein and it tends to carry cholesterol away from the cells. This is important in preventing a buildup of fatty deposits along the artery walls (atherosclerosis), the major cause of coronary artery disease. Thus, HDL cholesterol is referred to as the "good" or beneficial cholesterol; the higher the proportion of HDL cholesterol the better.

Low-density lipoprotein, or LDL, is lighter than HDL, and it appears to carry cholesterol to the cells. When there is excessive LDL cholesterol circulating in the blood, atherosclerosis is a common consequence. The lower the LDL the better.

There is a third lipoprotein, very-low-density lipoprotein or VLDL. It carries a large amount of triglycerides and is important in the production of other lipoproteins. It is not known if VLDL plays a role in the development of heart disease.

The goals of any heart-healthy eating program are to lower total cholesterol and to have as low a ratio of LDL to HDL cholesterol as possible. These are best accomplished by losing any excess weight, reducing the amount of total fat consumed to no more than 30 percent of calories evenly divided among saturated, monounsaturated, and polyunsaturated fats; increasing physical activity, which increases HDL cholesterol; and stopping smoking, which lowers LDL cholesterol.

The following "Simplified Weight Control Diet," food lists, cooking tips, and other materials have been developed specifically by Cleveland Clinic dietitians as part of a dietary approach to treating cardiovascular disease. Of course, before embarking on any diet change, it is important to check with your doctor. Expert guidance and counseling by a dietitian or qualified nutritionist experienced in working with hypertensive patients are also advisable.

THE CLEVELAND CLINIC'S SIMPLIFIED WEIGHT CONTROL DIET*

(Prepared by the Department of Dietetics—Clinical)

Weight control really means calorie control. Calories are a measurement of energy.

Your body uses energy for two processes:

1) Continuing body functions, such as heartbeat, breathing, digestion, etc., and
2) Physical activity—anything that requires voluntary muscular work.

Your body supplies itself with energy from the food you eat. Protein, carbohydrate, fat, and alcohol all have calories. If the calories you eat exceed the calories you use, your body stores the excess as fat. Likewise, if the calories you eat fall short, your body "burns" fat to make up the difference, resulting in weight loss.

Practically all foods contain calories. This means any food is "fattening" if you eat enough of it. Most people can lose weight simply by cutting down on serving sizes, while also avoiding high-calorie desserts and snacks.

This diet will help you do exactly that. It will also eliminate the need for counting calories. Instead, it will introduce you to a simple system of food groups that is easier to use.

In addition, this diet is designed to include a wide variety of foods, which will provide the vitamins, minerals, and other nutrients you need to stay healthy.

Remember the following:

1) Try to avoid using sugar, candy, honey, jam, jelly, preserves, marmalade, syrup, molasses, and any foods prepared with these items. These items add calories to the diet and are often not readily recognized in foods (for example, molasses in baked beans; sugar in sweetened fruit-flavored yogurt). If you feel that you will be eating these items on a daily basis, ask your dietitian to include these in your meal plan. (Cookies, candy, cakes and other such "sweets" also are very high in calories.)
2) Discuss the use of alcohol with your physician and nutritionist. (Alcohol stimulates the appetite and also may contribute to high blood pressure.)

---

* Note: This is a general weight-loss diet. Hypertensive patients may need to adjust it to lower sodium intake according to guidelines in chapter 6.

3) Purchase lean cuts of meat and trim all visible fat before cooking. Bake, broil, or roast meat on a rack.
4) Avoid fried foods, unless they are prepared with the fat allowance in your meal plan. Sauté foods with a minimum of fat.
5) Acquaint yourself with food labeling. When reading labels, remember that the word "dietetic" does not necessarily mean the food is lower in calories or is sugar-free.

Re-establishing new eating habits and patterns will help you not only to lose weight but also to maintain the weight loss. Try the following:

1) Keep a written record of everything you eat for a day, then count the number of servings from each of the six food groups listed below. Compare your tally with the number of servings recommended by your nutritionist to see how well your eating pattern coincides.
2) Plan a snack, using allowances from your meal plan, for the time of day you are most tempted to "nibble," for example: coffee break, midafternoon, or evening.
3) Eat slowly and chew thoroughly. This way, you can feel more satisfied with smaller portions.

MEAL PLAN

The following guideline to food selection makes it easy to plan meals providing the desired number of calories each day. Foods are grouped according to their nutritive and caloric values. Serving sizes are outlined in the following section. Note that two or more "servings" of a food may be eaten at one time, as long as the daily totals for each group agree with the meal plan. For example, if you are allowed five servings of meat per day, you may choose to have a five-ounce steak as your *only* selection from this group on one day. The next day you may choose one egg plus two ounces of cheese plus two ounces of chicken.

1) MEAT, FISH, POULTRY, EGGS, CHEESE
   75 calories per serving

   _____ servings per day.

2) STARCHY FOODS
   70 calories per serving

   _____ servings per day.
   Include products that are whole grain, enriched or restored.

3) FRUITS
   40 calories per serving

   _____ servings per day.
   Include one serving of citrus fruit or juice each day.

4) VEGETABLES   2 or more servings per day.
   25 calories per serving   Include one serving of dark green
                                 or yellow vegetable each day.

5) MILK   _____ servings per day.
   Skim milk: 90 calories per
   serving
   2%-fat milk: 125 calories per
   serving

6) FAT   _____ servings per day.
   45 calories per serving

FOOD GROUP/ SERVING SIZE	FOODS ALLOWED	FOODS TO AVOID
1) MEATS AND MEAT SUBSTITUTES ____ servings per day		
1 serving = 1 ounce (weight after cooking)	Beef, lamb, pork, veal, poultry, fish and shellfish; cold cuts, cheese.	Meats or meat substitutes prepared with a sweetened sauce; meats or meat substitutes in cream sauce; fried meats or meat substitutes.
1/4 cup	Cottage cheese, cooked dried beans, lentils, canned tuna or salmon.	
1	Egg	
1 tablespoon	Peanut butter	
2) STARCHY FOODS ____ servings per day		
1 serving = 1 slice	White, whole wheat, rye; French or Italian breads; bagels, biscuits, crackers, plain muffins, plain rolls, pancakes, waffles.	Doughnuts, pastries, sweet muffins and rolls.
1/2 cup	Dry (unsweetened), instant (unsweetened), or regular cooked cereals.	Sweetened dry cereals; instant cereals with sugar added.
1/2 cup	All white potatoes, sweet potatoes; rice, macaroni, noodles, spaghetti and other pastas; peas, lima	All potatoes and potato substitutes prepared with sugar; all potatoes and substitutes in cream

2) STARCHY FOODS (contd.)

	beans, corn, popcorn, pretzels.	sauce; all fried potatoes, potato chips.
1 cup	Soup—any type.	None.

DESSERTS (Limit to 2 per week)

1 serving = 1 slice, 1/2″ thick	Plain cake such as sponge, angel food, pound.	All pies; all other cakes with or without frostings; pastries.
1/2 cup	Ice cream, ice milk, low calorie pudding, regular gelatin or sherbet.	
3	Small shortbread cookies, gingersnaps, or vanilla wafers.	

3) FRUITS
_____ servings per day

1 serving = 1 small piece	Fresh fruit	All sweetened juices; all fruits canned in sugar or syrup, all sweetened frozen fruits.
1/2 cup	Unsweetened juice, unsweetened canned fruit, or fruit canned in fruit juice.	

4) VEGETABLES
2 or more servings per day

1 serving = 1/2 cup	Any fresh, frozen, or canned vegetables not listed as a potato substitute or under "FOODS TO AVOID."	All vegetables prepared with sweetened sauces; all creamed or fried vegetables.

5) MILK
_____ servings per day

1 serving = 1 cup	Low-fat milk, skim milk, buttermilk, reconstituted evaporated skim milk, or nonfat dry milk; plain yogurt made from whole or low-fat milk; low-calorie milk drinks (e.g., Alba).	All flavored milks; milk shakes, sweetened condensed milk; all flavored or fruited yogurt.

FOOD GROUP/ SERVING SIZE	FOODS ALLOWED	FOODS TO AVOID
6) FATS ____ servings per day 1 serving = 1 teaspoon	Butter, margarine, oil, shortening; cream cheese.	Any fats in excess of daily allowance.
1 tablespoon	Sour cream, cream or cream substitute, salad dressing, gravy.	

MISCELLANEOUS	FOODS ALLOWED (AS DESIRED)	FOODS TO AVOID
BAKING INGREDIENTS	Baking soda, baking powder, flavoring extracts, etc.	
BEVERAGES	Plain coffee, tea, decaffeinated coffee, sugar-free carbonated beverages, soda water, sugar-free Kool-Aid, sugar-free lemonade, sugar-free tonic water, mineral water.	Regular carbonated beverages, sweetened soda, fruit drinks, and all other sweetened beverages.
SWEETS	Sugar substitute; artificially sweetened jelly, jam, and syrup; low-calorie gelatin.	Sugar, brown sugar, powdered sugar; candy, dietetic candy; honey, jelly, jam, preserves, marmalades, syrup, molasses.

SHOPPING POINTERS

Read labels carefully before buying any packaged food. Most foods can be purchased at your regular grocery store. It is seldom necessary to go to a health food store. Avoid frozen dinners or other ready-to-eat canned food mixtures containing fat. You have no way of knowing the type of fat used.

Package mixes and dehydrated foods such as potatoes or pancake mixes to which you add the fat yourself are usually all right. Avoid commercially baked goods or mixes with coconut or palm oils, which are highly saturated fats.

SUBSTITUTIONS WHEN COOKING

RECIPE CALLS FOR:	USE INSTEAD:
1 egg yolk	1 egg white
1 whole egg	2 egg whites
2 eggs	3 egg whites
Cheese	Dry cottage cheese or cheese made from skim milk
	Sapsago for grating
Cream	Powdered skim milk mixed to double or triple strength
Milk	Skim milk
Butter or shortening	Low-fat margarine or oil

COOKING TIPS

MEATS

Meat fat is saturated fat, therefore, cooking should be geared to removing as much fat from the meat as practical. When broiling, baking, browning, or roasting meat, use a rack so excess fat can drain off. Meat can be kept moist by adding wine, tomato juice, broth, or even water over it. Oil may be used, and in combination with some spices and herbs makes a really tasty meat. Keep the drippings. The next day, after the fat has hardened, remove it and use drippings for gravy or sauces.

Other foods to be cooked a day ahead of time include soups, stews, boiled meats, and combination dishes. All hardened fat can be removed. It is best to broil rather than panfry hamburgers, chops, and steaks.

VEGETABLES

Vegetables can be prepared in your usual way with low-fat margarine or oil substituted for butter.

Herbs and spices can do a great deal to enhance the flavor of vegetables. Try sweet basil with tomatoes, rosemary with peas, etc. There are many variations.

Vegetables can be steamed or prepared in vegetable oil, using little or no water in a covered pot. Use about 1 to 2 teaspoons oil per serving. Use very low heat.

COOKING WITH OIL

Liquid vegetable oils are excellent for sautéing, frying, and general cookery. Use oil for the following:

For sautéing onions, garlic, or other vegetables

For making hot breads, pie crust, and cake

For popping corn

For pancakes and waffles

For browning rice

SELECTING A MARGARINE

Only margarines containing large amounts of unhydrogenated, liquid vegetable oil are suitable for your diet. Check the label carefully. The first ingredient listed on the label should be liquid oil.

Acceptable brands include Promise, Emdee, Saffola, Award, Mazola, and Fleischman's.

Low-calorie margarines are low in fat, and therefore it takes twice the amount to equal 1 tablespoon of oil.

SAMPLE MENUS

I	II
BREAKFAST	
Banana	Orange juice
Cornflakes	Homemade pancakes
Toast	Margarine
Margarine	Syrup
Jelly	Skim milk
Skim milk	Coffee or tea
Coffee or tea	

LUNCH

Cottage cheese 1/2 cup	Sandwich: sliced turkey with 2 oz.
Sliced tomato	mayonnaise

Hard roll
Margarine
Fresh fruit cup
Skim milk
Coffee or tea

Tossed salad with vinegar and oil
Fruited Jell-O
Skim milk
Coffee or tea

DINNER

Roast beef, 3 oz.
Mashed potato
Broccoli
Tossed salad with French
    dressing
Bread and margarine
Orange sherbet
Skim milk
Coffee or tea

Baked whitefish, 4 oz.
Baked potato with
    margarine
Green beans
Coleslaw
Bread and margarine
Angel food cake
Skim milk
Coffee or tea

RESTAURANT SUGGESTIONS

SAMPLE MENU III

BREAKFAST

Grapefruit half
1 Poached egg*
Toast
Margarine
Skim milk
Coffee or tea

LUNCH

Tomato juice
Tuna salad sandwich
Fresh grapes
Skim milk
Coffee or tea

DINNER

Veal cutlet, 3 1/2 oz.
Escalloped potato

APPETIZERS:

Consommé, fruit cup, tomato or fruit
    juice

ENTREES:

Lean meat, chicken or fish, baked or
    broiled.
Do not eat breading or skin on chicken
    or fish

VEGETABLE OR POTATO:

No added fat. Special margarine if
    available

SALADS:

Vegetable or fruit salad with salad
    dressing, vinegar and oil or

Corn
Fresh fruit salad
Mayonnaise
Bread
Margarine
Special pudding
Skim milk

mayonnaise. (Avoid dressings containing cheese or egg.)

BREAD OR HARD ROLLS:

With jelly or special margarine

SANDWICHES:

Sliced white meat of chicken, beef, veal, turkey, baked ham or lean corned beef. (Trim fat off.) Chicken or tuna salad sandwich (no egg). Peanut butter and jelly.

Lettuce and tomato, mayonnaise (no bacon).

Frankfurter or hamburger sandwich occasionally (select a low-fat meat at your evening meal)

DESSERTS:

Fruited gelatin, fresh or canned fruit, angel food cake (unfrosted)

* Eggs are limited to 2 a week.

RECIPES

Breaded Veal Cutlet

2 tbsp. bread crumbs
1 tbsp. chopped parsley
  Salt and pepper to taste
1/2 clove finely minced garlic
  (optional)

2 slices veal steak
  (about 4 oz. each)
1 egg white, slightly beaten
  with 1 tbsp. skim milk
2 tbsp. oil

Combine bread crumbs with parsley and seasonings. Dip veal in egg white and then in crumbs. Heat oil in skillet. Sauté veal on both sides until done. Makes 2 servings.

VEAL SCALOPPINE

2 tbsp. vegetable oil
1 lb. veal cutlet, sliced thin
    and cut into 2-inch pieces
1 cup mushrooms, sliced

1 tbsp. minced onion
1 tbsp. chopped parsley or mint
    Salt and pepper to taste
1/4 cup Marsala or Sherry wine

Heat oil in skillet. Brown veal quickly. Remove from pan. Brown mushrooms and onion in same skillet. Return meat to skillet. Add seasonings and wine. Cover and simmer for 10 minutes. Serves 4.

CHICKEN OR TURKEY TETRAZZINI

1/4 lb. fresh mushrooms, sliced
1/4 cup special margarine
1/4 cup flour
2 cups chicken broth (fat free)
2 tbsp. sherry

1 cup skim milk
    Salt and pepper to taste
1 8-oz. pkg. spaghetti, cooked
2 cups diced chicken or turkey
1/3 cup bread crumbs

Preheat oven to 400° F. Brown mushrooms in margarine. Stir in flour. Add broth, sherry, and skim milk, salt and pepper. Arrange layers of spaghetti, chicken, and mushroom sauce alternately in a greased 2-quart casserole. Cover with bread crumbs. Bake about 20 minutes. Serves 4.

OVEN BARBECUED CHICKEN

2 tbsp. chopped onion
3 tbsp. vegetable oil
1/4 cup water
1/4 cup vinegar
1/2 cup chili sauce
1 tbsp. Worcestershire sauce

1 tsp. dry mustard
2 tsp. salt
1 tsp. pepper
1 frying chicken 2 1/2 lbs.
    cut into serving pieces

Preheat oven to 350° F. Sauté onion in vegetable oil for 10 minutes. Add remaining ingredients except chicken and simmer 10 minutes. Remove skin from chicken. Place chicken in large baking pan. Pour half the sauce over chicken and bake for 1 hour. Baste with remaining sauce during cooking. Serves 4.

Fish Chowder

3 tbsp. vegetable oil
1 medium onion, chopped
1 8-oz. can tomatoes
2 tsp. salt
  Pepper to taste
1 tsp. sweet basil

1 medium potato, diced
1 cup water
1 lb. fish fillets such as
  cod or haddock
6 green olives (optional)

Heat oil in skillet. Brown onion. Add tomatoes, salt, pepper, and basil. Let simmer 15 minutes. Mash tomato with fork to remove chunks, add diced potato and water. Cook 15 more minutes. Add fish and olives and enough water to cover. Cook about 15 more minutes. Serves 4.

Beef Bourguignon

2 tbsp. oil
5 medium onions, sliced
2 lbs. lean beef cubes
1 1/2 tbsp. flour
  Marjoram, thyme, salt and
  pepper to taste

1/2 cup bouillon, plus more if
  needed
1 cup dry red wine, plus more if
  needed
1/2 lb. sliced fresh mushrooms

Heat oil in skillet. Brown onions, remove onions to another dish and brown beef in remaining oil. Sprinkle meat with flour and seasonings. Add 1/2 cup bouillon and 1 cup dry red wine. Stir mixture well. Simmer for 1 1/2 to 2 hours, very slowly. Add more bouillon and wine (1 part bouillon to 2 parts wine) as necessary to keep beef barely covered.

Return onions to skillet, add mushrooms, cook 30 minutes longer. Add more bouillon and wine mixture if necessary. Sauce should be thick and dark brown. Makes 8 servings (1 serving equals 3 oz. beef and 1 tsp. oil).

Fried Potato Slices

1/4 cup vegetable oil
 2 medium potatoes, peeled and sliced 1/4 inch thick
  Salt and pepper to taste

Heat oil in skillet. Arrange potato slices, a few at a time in skillet so they do not overlap. Sprinkle with salt and pepper. Brown on one side, turn over and brown other side. Remove from skillet. Repeat process until all slices are browned. Serves 4.

FRENCH SALAD DRESSING

3/4 cup vinegar	*1 tbsp. salt*
1 10 1/2-oz. can tomato soup	*1 tsp. paprika*
3/4 cup oil	*1 tbsp. mustard*
1/3 cup sugar	*1 tbsp. Worcestershire sauce*
1 tsp. pepper	*1 tbsp. onion juice*

Combine all ingredients and mix well. Makes 3 1/2 cups.

VINEGAR AND OIL DRESSING

1/2 cup vegetable oil	*2 tsp. salt*
1/4 cup vinegar	*1 tsp. pepper*
1 tbsp. minced onion	

Combine all ingredients in a jar. Put on lid and shake well. Save in refrigerator and use as needed. Shake before using.

PANCAKES OR WAFFLES

1/2 tsp. salt	*2 tsp. baking powder*
2 egg whites	*3/4 cup skim milk*
3/4 cup flour	*2 tbsp. oil*

Sprinkle dash of salt on whites. Beat until stiff but not dry. Sift together dry ingredients. Add skim milk gradually to dry ingredients. Add oil. Fold in beaten egg whites. Cook in waffle iron or on griddle. Makes 15 pancakes or 10 waffles.

FRENCH TOAST

1 egg white	*Pinch of salt*
2 tbsp. skim milk	*2 slices bread*

Mix egg white, milk, and salt. Beat. Dip bread into egg mixture. Brown in frying pan with vegetable oil.

Pizza

6 cups flour
1 tbsp. salt
2 1/2 cups lukewarm water
1 pkg. yeast dissolved
  in 1/2 cup warm water
1 tbsp. oil

1 small onion
1/4 cup oil
2 small cans tomato sauce
1 tbsp. sweet basil
1/4 cup oregano
Salt and pepper to taste

Combine flour, 1 tbsp. salt, water, and yeast all at once. Knead to make a smooth dough. If sticky, add a little more flour. Rub outside of dough and bowl with 1 tbsp. oil. Let rise until double in bulk—about 2 hours. Divide dough in half and roll out into two round pizzas. Cut up onion and brown in 1/4 cup oil. Add tomato sauce, sweet basil, salt and pepper to taste. Simmer for 15 minutes. Spread sauce on pizza and sprinkle with oregano.

Bake at 400° F. for 20 to 25 minutes. Serves 4 to 6.

Two-Crust Pie Dough

2 cups flour
1/2 tsp. salt
1/4 tsp. baking powder

1/2 cup oil
1/4 cup water

Sift together dry ingredients. Mix in oil and water. Form into two balls. Roll out between two sheets of waxed paper. Fill as desired.

Pineapple Ice

1 cup sugar
1 1/2 cups water
Dash salt

2 cups pineapple juice
1/2 cup lemon juice
2 egg whites

Boil sugar, water, salt for 2 minutes. Add pineapple and lemon juices. Freeze in refrigerator tray until mushy. Beat until smooth. Beat egg whites until stiff and fold into above mixture. Freeze until firm, stirring once. Serves 4 to 6.

Apple Crisp

1 cup sliced raw apple	1 graham cracker, crumbled
1 tsp. lemon juice	1/8 tsp. cinnamon
2 tbsp. brown sugar	1 tbsp. margarine

Preheat oven to 375° F. Sprinkle apple slices with lemon juice. Mix remaining ingredients. Alternate apples and crumb mixture in individual casseroles. Bake for 30 to 35 minutes. Serve warm. Serves 2.

White Layer Cake

2 cups cake flour	1 cup sugar
3 tsp. baking powder	1/2 cup oil
3/4 tsp. salt	1 cup skim milk less 2 tbsp.
3 egg whites	1 tsp. vanilla extract
1/4 cup sugar	1/2 tsp. almond extract

Preheat oven to 375° F. Sift together flour, baking powder, and salt. Beat egg whites until foamy. Add 1/4 cup sugar, beat until stiff. Combine 1 cup sugar and 1/2 cup oil and beat with mixer until light and fluffy. Combine milk and extracts. Add this to oil mixture alternately with the flour mixture. Fold in egg whites. Pour into greased, paper-lined pan 9" × 9" × 2". Bake for 30 to 35 minutes.

Fluffy White Frosting

2/3 cup sugar	2 egg whites
1/3 cup water	

Boil sugar and water together until syrupy—about 10 minutes. Beat egg whites until firm. Add hot syrup gradually while beating. Frosts one cake.

Vegetable Oil Cream

1 cup cold water	4 tbsp. vegetable oil
1/3 cup powdered skim milk	2–3 drops butter flavor or vanilla extract

Combine all ingredients. Put in blender, beat at high speed for 2 minutes. Chill. Use in any recipe that calls for cream.

Strawberry Ice Cream

1 tbsp. gelatin	2 cups vegetable oil cream
1/4 cup cold water	(recipe above)
1 3/4 cup skim milk	1/4 tsp. salt
1/2 cup sugar	1/2 cup mashed strawberries

Soften gelatin in cold water. Scald milk in double boiler. Dissolve softened gelatin in milk. Add sugar and stir. Add cream. Add salt and strawberries. Freeze in refrigerator or freezer. Serves 4 to 6.

6
Salt and Hypertension

INTRODUCTION

Although drugs are the major treatment for hypertension, diet plays a vital role in treatment and may also play a role in prevention for some people with a hereditary predisposition to high blood pressure. Weight reduction is essential for hypertensives who are more than 20 percent overweight, as is reduction in fat and cholesterol intake for all those with high blood lipids. (Guidelines for control of calories, fat, and cholesterol are given in chapter 5.)

The other major dietary modification most high blood pressure patients must make is to control sodium intake. For most people, this is easier than they first imagine, and many find it far easier than losing weight. Many people who successfully control their sodium intake eventually find they are able to control their blood pressure with less medication, and some are even able to forgo drugs completely.

A small amount of sodium, about one half to one gram daily, is necessary for the proper functioning of the body. Sodium is an essential nutrient; specifically, it is an electrolyte. Sodium is needed to regulate the amount of water retained by the body and this in turn is necessary to maintain the appropriate volume and consistency of the blood. The kidneys act as the body's regulator of sodium. When there is too much, they filter it out and the excess is excreted in the urine. When there is not enough, they reabsorb sodium from the urine and return it to the blood.

When the kidneys fail to excrete enough sodium, and the body retains too much water, blood volume increases. This excess blood circulating through the vessels makes them overly sensitive to nerve stimulation that causes them to constrict. Now more blood must pass through even narrower vessels, which raises blood pressure. The pulse rate also increases, because the heart is working harder to pump more blood. To compensate, the blood vessels constrict even more, further building up the pressure until it is too high. Thus, cutting down on salt relieves some of the pressure on the kidneys, the heart, and the blood vessels.

For reasons that are not completely understood, some people are particularly sensitive to the effects of sodium. Studies have shown that newborns and infants do not like the taste of salt, preferring sugar—a taste that is thought to hark back to our early foraging ancestors who quickly learned that sweet-tasting fruits and plants are less likely to be poisonous than those that are bitter or sour.

Humans have four basic tastes—salt, sweet, sour, and bitter. A taste for salt is essential, since a small amount of sodium is essential to maintain life. As humans evolved, a complex internal system developed to conserve salt and to excrete potassium, another essential electrolyte that was more abundant than sodium in early diets. Salt was a scarce commodity in early times—people who lived away from the sea often had difficulty obtaining it. Wars have been fought for salt, and for some early societies, salt was more precious than gold.

Today, of course, the situation is reversed; sodium is abundant in industrialized societies, but potassium is lacking in many diets. Unfortunately, the body is still geared to conserve sodium and excrete potassium. If a person has a genetic tendency to hypertension, high blood pressure is likely to develop if the diet provides excessive salt. Many of these people develop a craving for salt, especially if it is added to their diet at an early age.

So, although most people can consume large amounts of salt with impunity, others cannot without developing high blood pressure. These people are advised to restrict sodium as part of their antihypertensive regimen. Most find that their craving for salt will wane after three to six weeks on a sodium-restricted diet. Within that amount of time, foods that tasted normal before will begin to taste too salty.

HOW MUCH SODIUM IS TOO MUCH?

The actual physiological need for sodium may be as low as 220 milligrams a day, although the Recommended Dietary Allowance for adults with normal blood pressure is much higher, 1,100 to 3,300 milligrams. Most Americans consume much more than that—2,400 to 8,000 milligrams daily, or the amount in about one to three teaspoons of salt.

A mildly restricted sodium intake might allow 2,000 milligrams (or one teaspoon) a day, while moderate restriction would be 1,000 milligrams (or half a teaspoon). A very restricted diet may be set at 500 milligrams, about a quarter of a teaspoon. But these examples are not standard guidelines, and what is recommended for an individual patient may vary.

In practical terms, patients on a mildly restricted diet usually need to cut in half the amount of salt, monosodium glutamate (MSG), and other sources of sodium normally used in cooking and at the table, and salt should not be added to any product that already contains it. In addition, patients should avoid highly salted foods (see the Cleveland Clinic list in Table 6.1), but most will not have to worry about counting milligrams or buying low-sodium products, or avoiding foods that contain only moderate amounts of sodium. Very few hypertensive patients are now placed on severely restrictive low-sodium diets, thanks to the advent of antihypertensive drugs that can effectively lower blood pressure and prevent excessive sodium retention.

For patients on a moderately restricted diet, about half the allowed sodium intake comes from eating a balanced diet but substituting low-sodium breads, cereals, and fat (such as margarine). Highly salted foods must be avoided (see Table 6.1). The remaining allowed sodium can come from adding small amounts of salt or MSG in cooking or at the table, limiting high-sodium food to only occasional small amounts. Remember, most sodium is consumed in processed foods. Fast foods usually are very high in sodium, as well as calories and fats, and should be avoided.

Patients on a very restricted diet can enjoy the same balanced diet as those on a moderate restriction but should not add any salt or MSG in cooking or at the table and should not eat any high-sodium foods.

SOURCES OF SODIUM AND POTASSIUM

Sodium is most commonly found in table salt, a compound of sodium and chloride (NaCl). The average American adult consumes anywhere from 6 to 20 grams of sodium chloride daily, or as much as 15 pounds a year. Since sodium chloride is 40 percent sodium, actual consumption is 2.4 to 8 grams a day, still many more times the necessary requirement. In addition to reducing sodium intake, most experts agree it is also a good idea to increase consumption of foods high in potassium, such as those listed in Table 6.2.

Although most people are aware of the obvious sources of sodium—the salt in the salt shaker and foods that taste salty, such as olives, anchovies, ham, soy sauce, and the like—there are dozens of sources of hidden sodium. It turns up in many forms as a preservative and flavor and texture enhancer in processed foods and even in many over-the-counter medications. The following list gives common sources of sodium in food:

- Monosodium glutamate (MSG)—a tenderizer and seasoning used in cooking and preserving foods. It is commonly found in Chinese dishes, but many home cooks and restaurants use it to season everything from meats to vegetables.
- Baking soda (sodium bicarbonate or bicarbonate of soda)—used to leaven

breads and cakes; sometimes added to vegetables in cooking to keep them bright green. It also has many household uses, from antacid to dentifrice.

- Baking powder (baking soda plus acid)—used to leaven quick breads, muffins, and cakes.
- Brine—table salt and water used to flavor corned beef, pickles, and sauerkraut, as well as to preserve vegetables and condiments such as artichokes, olives, capers, etc. Since it inhibits the growth of bacteria and controls insects, it is commonly used in processing foods and in washing fruits and vegetables.
- Disodium phosphate—used in some quick-cooking cereals and processed cheese and meat to retain liquids.
- Sodium alginate—used in many chocolate milks and ice creams for smooth texture.
- Sodium benzoate—found as a preservative in many condiments, such as relishes, sauces, and salad dressings.
- Sodium hydroxide—used in food processing to soften and loosen skins of ripe olives, hominy, and certain fruits and vegetables.
- Sodium nitrate and sodium nitrite—both used to cure meats and sausages.
- Sodium propionate—used in pasteurized cheeses and in some breads and cakes to inhibit growth of mold.
- Sodium sulfite—used to bleach certain fruits in which an artificial color is desired, such as maraschino cherries and glazed or crystallized fruit; also used as a preservative in some dried fruit, such as prunes.
- Sodium cyclamate and sodium saccharin—used in some low-calorie soft drinks and desserts.
- Whey solids—the liquid drained off from yogurt, used as filler.
- Sodium ascorbate—used as a preservative.
- Sodium citrate—used as a flavoring.
- Hydrolyzed vegetable protein—used as a filler.
- Soy sauce and soy isolates—used as flavoring.
- Dry skim milk—used in a number of products, including baked goods.

DRINKING WATER

Drinking water can be an important source of sodium, especially if commercial water softeners are used. If local water supplies have a high-sodium content, and a person is on a very restricted low-sodium diet, drinking water may be a source that needs to be considered. Local health departments, municipal water departments, or water companies can determine the sodium

TABLE 6.1. WATCH YOUR INTAKE OF SODIUM

CHOOSE	LIMIT OR AVOID
Fruits and Juices	Cured or processed meats:
Fresh Meats: *Beef, pork, veal, lamb, chicken, turkey, fish*	*Bacon, ham, corned beef, sausage, hot dogs, luncheon meats, meat spreads, regular canned meat or fish*
Eggs	
Butter	Cheeses
Margarine	Soups:
Mayonnaise	*Regular, canned, dry or instant soups, broths or bouillon*
Vinegar and Oil	Sauces and Condiments:
Breads, Cereals	*Pickles, olives, catsup, mustard, salad dressings, steak sauce, barbecue sauce, soy sauce, Worcestershire sauce, spaghetti sauce, sauerkraut, packaged gravy mixes, seasoned salts*
Noodles, Rice	
Vegetables: *Any fresh, frozen, or canned without salt*	
Soups, Stews, Casseroles: *Homemade without salt, or canned low-sodium*	Frozen or Boxed Mixes for: *Potato, rice, pasta casseroles*
Unsalted Snacks: *Popcorn, pretzels, nuts, crackers, chips*	Salted Snacks: *Popcorn, pretzels, chips, nuts, dips, crackers*
Low-sodium Cheese	TV dinners
Herbs and Spices: *Without salt added*	Pot pies
Desserts	

content of drinking water. Individual wells or springs can be analyzed by a local water department, county agent, or independent laboratory.

Agents used to soften water for household use usually contain sodium; softened water for drinking or cooking should be avoided by people who need to watch their sodium intake. Bottled water also may contain sodium. Some

TABLE 6.2. SOURCES OF POTASSIUM

VERY GOOD SOURCES

Banana (1 medium)
Cantaloupe (1 cup)
Prunes (10 medium)
Grapefruit, orange, or tomato juice (1 cup)
Prune juice (1 cup)
White potato (1 medium)

GOOD SOURCES

1/2 cup of any of these:
    Cooked dried beans
    Cooked greens
    Canned tomatoes
    Sweet potato
    Lima beans
    Mashed white potato
    Winter squash

Fresh tomato (1 medium)
Orange (1 small)
Watermelon (2 cups)
Raisins (1/3 cup)

Skim milk and low-fat buttermilk (1 cup)
Nonfat dry milk powder (1/4 cup)
Apple juice (1 cup)
Peaches (1 whole)
Fruit cocktail (1/2 cup)
Unsalted peanuts (1/4 cup)

---

natural spring water is low in sodium, but some "mineral water" is not. Seltzer is generally low in sodium, while club soda, with salt added, is not. Some doctors may recommend distilled water instead. If the sodium content is not listed on bottled water, the patient should write to the manufacturer for this information.

Since soft drinks, even national brands, are bottled regionally, they may also vary in sodium content, depending on the local water supply.

SODIUM IN THE MEDICINE CHEST

A number of over-the-counter medications contain various forms of sodium, as do prescription antibiotics, pain relievers, and sedatives. Hypertensive patients should always tell the doctors they are seeing for other conditions that they are on a sodium-restricted diet so that if drugs are needed, low-sodium ones can be prescribed. When choosing over-the-counter medications, patients should check with their doctor or pharmacist. Here are the most common preparations containing sodium:

- Antacids—Many of them contain sodium bicarbonate, sodium citrate, or sodium phosphate. Instead, choose brands that use magnesium hydroxide, aluminum hydroxide, or calcium carbonate. The sodium content must be stated on the label if it is 5 milligrams or more per dose (e.g., tablet, tablespoon). Some popular brands are now available in a low-sodium formula.
- Laxatives—Many of these also contain sodium bicarbonate, sodium phosphate, and sodium citrate.
- Sleeping pills—Some contain sodium citrate.
- Vitamin C—This is usually found in the form of ascorbic acid, which is acceptable, but sodium ascorbate forms should be avoided.
- Toothpastes, tooth powders, and mouthwashes may also contain large amounts of sodium, but they are not a problem unless swallowed.

SHOPPING

Shopping may take a little longer in the beginning, until patients can identify items and brands that are within acceptable limits. The two main rules for shopping: Use as many fresh products as possible and read the labels of all processed foods.

Sodium occurs naturally in many foods—an average egg contains 60 milligrams; a cup of whole milk has 122; a stalk of celery has 25—but these quantities are not a problem for most people. As a rule, fresh fruits have very little, fresh vegetables only a bit more (with a few exceptions). Milk, eggs, and fresh meat are relatively high but, because they provide many essential nutrients, they are included in even the most restrictive diets.

Add commercial food processing, however, and the sodium usually soars. For example, a cup of cooked fresh corn contains only 1 milligram of sodium, while a cup of frozen has 7, and a cup of canned has a whopping 671. Three ounces of fresh shrimp contains about 137 milligrams of sodium, while the same amount canned contains 1,955.

Next to fresh foods, frozen products are best, assuming they are frozen in their natural state, not coated with sauce or cooked into complete dinners. TV dinners and boil-in-bag vegetables should be avoided. Canned foods are, for the most part, a poor third. So, too, are packaged dinners and other prepared mixes. Categorically, the worst bets are snack foods, especially crackers and chips. But, fortunately, this is an area where many manufacturers are developing low-sodium product lines.

To avoid products that are highly salted, learn the list of common forms of sodium on pp. 69–70. Remember that any compound with the word sodium or soda in it should alert you.

Many products are now listing sodium content along with other nutritional information, either in grams or milligrams per serving. On labels where amounts are not specified, convention dictates that ingredients be listed in descending order by quantity. Sodium may appear in several forms in any one food; individually, they may all appear toward the end of the list, but when added together, sodium may become a major ingredient.

Since not only hypertensives, but the American public as a whole has been cutting down on sodium intake, manufacturers have responded with many new or reformulated products that are low or lower in sodium. These tend, however, to be higher in price than conventional canned food, so compare the low-sodium against fresh produce before you buy.

The FDA currently requires that foods sold as low-sodium items must list on the label the number of milligrams per serving. As of July 1986, any product that carries a nutrition label must also contain sodium information. Nutrition labeling is required on certain categories of products, including any that make a nutritional claim (such as "dietetic" or "fortified") or that have added vitamins or minerals. In addition, a growing number of manufacturers and processors voluntarily use nutritional labeling, or make the information available on request.

Although the FDA has set standards for what constitutes low sodium, some forms of labeling are not yet uniform. For example, the term "lite" on many new products can refer to a reduction of calories, fat, or sodium. This is a relative, rather than an absolute term. To be labeled "lite," a product need only contain a lower amount of calories, fat, or sodium than the original product. Patients shouldn't assume it is safe to use, since it may still contain too much sodium, or it may be reduced only in calories or fat.

INTERPRETING FOOD LABELS

The Food and Drug Administration has established the following criteria for food labeling regarding sodium content:

When the label says:	It means:
Sodium free	less than 5 milligrams per serving
Very low sodium	35 milligrams or less per serving
Low sodium	140 milligrams or less per serving
Reduced sodium	processed to reduce the usual level of sodium by 75 percent
Unsalted	processed without the normally used salt

COOKING

Many people begin cooking without salt, thinking they must give up flavor, and soon discover the subtle flavors of the food itself or the dozens of herbs and spices they can use instead.

No lesser cooks than the late James Beard and New York *Times* food columnist and cookbook author Craig Claiborne have eliminated salt successfully. Claiborne, a self-confessed salt addict, gave it up almost overnight once he was diagnosed as a hypertensive. Beard had given it up for the same reason.

The first place to give up salt is at the table. Shaking salt on food—sometimes even without tasting the food first—is a habit. If you feel you must have something on the table, fill your salt shaker with one of the recipes on p. 76. Do *not* use a commercial salt substitute without discussing it with your doctor or nutrition counselor first. These commercial preparations generally contain potassium, which may be a problem for some patients with kidney disease or who are already taking a potassium supplement or a potassium-conserving medication. Many people find that these substitutes have a bitter aftertaste. Still other substitutes that use "natural ingredients" may contain such foods as spinach or beet greens, which are naturally high in sodium and not appropriate for many diets.

SALT SUBSTITUTE RECIPES

HERB SEASONING

2 tbsp. dried dillweed or
  basil leaves, crumbled
2 tbsp. onion powder
  (not onion salt)
1 tsp. dried oregano leaves,
  crumbled

1 tsp. celery seed
1/4 tsp. grated dried
  lemon peel
  Pinch of freshly ground
  pepper

SPICY BLEND I

2 tbsp. dried savory,
  crumbled
1 tbsp. dry mustard
2 1/2 tsp. onion powder
1 1/4 tsp. curry powder

1 1/4 tsp. freshly ground
  white pepper
1 1/4 tsp. ground cumin
1/2 tsp. garlic powder

SPICY BLEND II

1/2 tsp. cayenne pepper
1 tbsp. garlic powder
1 tsp. of each of the following, ground:

  basil   mace
  marjoram   onion powder
  thyme   black pepper
  rosemary   sage
  savory   cumin

For any of these recipes: Combine all ingredients in a small bowl and blend well. Spoon into a salt shaker with large holes. Store in a cool, dark place. Sprinkle liberally on meats, poultry, fish, vegetables, soups, and salads.

In addition to eliminating added table salt, salt in cooking also should be cut. Some salt can be eliminated completely, such as the tablespoon or more that is routinely added to water in which pasta or rice is cooked. Plain pasta without salt may be bland, but no one eats it absolutely plain. Once a sauce or herbs are added, the salt is not missed. Rice can be cooked with a number of herbs or spices in place of salt.

In virtually any dish, the salt, MSG, or soy sauce can be cut in half with little noticeable difference. Once a person becomes accustomed to this new level, the salt can be cut in half again, and then again. Whenever possible, the salt should be added at the end, after the dish has been tasted.

The most enjoyable—and easiest—way to cook, however, is not to be concerned with how much salt to add, but to eliminate it completely and begin experimenting with herbs (preferably fresh) and spices. Many herbs can be grown easily throughout the winter on a sunny windowsill, and more and more supermarkets and green grocers are stocking fresh herbs throughout the year. The list below gives some suggestions for using herbs and spices to flavor meats, poultry, fish, vegetables, soups, and casseroles. There are further suggestions in the cookbooks mentioned on p. 76.

Those who cook with wine should be sure to use table wine and not cooking wine, which has salt added. Inexpensive table wine is often the same price or less expensive than cooking wine. Decanting it into smaller containers will help it keep longer.

Although there are several brands of low-sodium soups on the market, it is not always easy to find low-sodium bouillon cubes or stocks. The recipes on pp. 79–81, from the American Heart Association's Culinary Hearts Kitchen cooking course, will provide stock that can be frozen in various quantities up to four months.

FLAVORING ALTERNATIVES

BEEF: allspice, basil, bay leaf, cardamom, chives, curry, garlic, lemon juice, mace, marjoram, mushrooms, mustard (dry), nutmeg, onion, oregano, paprika, parsley, pepper, green peppers, sage, savory, tarragon, thyme, turmeric, vinegar or wine for marinating.

CHICKEN OR TURKEY: allspice, apples, basil, bay leaf, cardamom, cranberries, cumin, curry, garlic, lemon, mace, marjoram, mushrooms, mustard (dry), oranges, paprika, parsley, pepper, pineapple, rosemary, sage, savory, tarragon, thyme, turmeric.

LAMB: basil, curry, dill, garlic, mace, marjoram, mint, onion, oregano, parsley, pepper, pineapple, rosemary, thyme, turmeric.

PORK: apples, basil, cardamom, cloves, cranberries, curry, dill, fruit juices, garlic, mace, marjoram, mustard (dry), onion, oregano, parsley, pepper, rosemary, sage, thyme, turmeric.

VEAL: apricots, basil, bay leaf, currants, curry, dill, garlic, ginger, mace, marjoram, oregano, paprika, parsley, peaches, pepper, rosemary, sage, savory, tarragon, thyme, turmeric.

FISH: bay leaf, chives, coriander, curry, dill, garlic, lemon or lime, mace, marjoram, mushrooms, mustard (dry), onion, oregano, paprika, parsley, pepper, green peppers, sage, savory, tarragon, thyme, turmeric.

LEGUMES (navy beans, etc.): strong herbs and spices such as garlic, onions, or scallions; basil, cumin, dill, mint, oregano, paprika, sage, thyme.

TOFU: strong herbs and spices such as chives, cilantro or Chinese parsley, dill, garlic or scallions, ginger, oregano. This product is very bland and will absorb a lot of flavor.

VEGETABLES

ASPARAGUS: caraway seed, lemon juice, mustard, unsalted chopped nuts, nutmeg, sesame seeds.

BEANS, GREEN: slivered almonds, basil, bay leaves, cinnamon, dill, lemon juice, mace, marjoram, nutmeg, onion, oregano, rosemary, sesame.

BROCCOLI: lemon juice, oregano, tarragon.

CABBAGE: basil, caraway seed, cinnamon, dill, mace, margarine with lemon and sugar, mustard (dry), nutmeg, savory, tarragon.

CARROTS: chili powder, cinnamon, ginger, mace, margarine, marjoram, mint, nutmeg, parsley, poppy seed, sugar, thyme.

CAULIFLOWER: caraway seeds, curry, dill, mace, nutmeg, rosemary, savory, tarragon.

CORN: chili powder, chives, curry, parsley, green peppers, pimiento, tomatoes.

PEAS: chili powder, cinnamon, dill, mace, marjoram, mint, mushrooms, mustard (dry), onion, oregano, parsley, green peppers, poppy seed, savory, thyme.

POTATOES: caraway seed, chives, dill, mace, margarine, mint, onion, oregano, parsley, green peppers, poppy seed, thyme.

SWEET POTATO: allspice, apples, brown sugar,* cardamom, cinnamon, ginger, nutmeg, orange slices, sugar.*

TOMATOES: basil, chives, dill, marjoram, onion, oregano, parsley, sage, sugar,* tarragon, thyme.

---

* If concentrated carbohydrates (because of diabetes) and/or calories are not restricted on your diet, you may use jam, jelly, honey, margarine, and low-sodium salad dressings.

A SAMPLING OF LOW-SODIUM COOKBOOKS

Cooking Without a Grain of Salt, Elma W. Bagg, Doubleday & Company, Garden City, N.Y., 1964. Also in Bantam Books paperback.

Cooking Without Your Salt Shaker, American Heart Association. Available through local AHA chapters.

The Dieter's Gourmet Cookbook, Francine Prince, Cornerstone Library, New York, N.Y., 1979.

Gourmet Cooking Without Salt, Eleanor P. Brenner, Doubleday & Company, Garden City, N.Y., 1981.

Salt-Free Cooking with Herbs and Spices, June Roth, Contemporary Books, Chicago, Ill., 1977.

The Sodium Content of Your Food, from the U.S. Department of Agriculture, is another helpful publication. It lists the sodium content of 789 foods and food products and is available for $2.25 from:

Superintendent of Documents
U.S. Government Printing Office
Washington, D.C. 20402
(Request publication number 001-000-04179-7.
Make check or money order payable to Superintendent of Documents.)

SALT-FREE CHICKEN OR TURKEY STOCK*

YIELD: 1 to 1¹/₂ quarts
APPROX. CAL.: 262

3 qts. (12 cups) water	*2 large onions, chopped*
3 lbs. uncooked chicken or turkey	*1 medium carrot, chopped*
bones (with some meat on them)†	*1 celery stalk, chopped*

Fresh herb bouquet garni: *1 sprig each parsley, thyme, basil, and marjoram; 1 bay leaf; celery tops from 1 stalk; 1 branch tarragon, 2 garlic cloves sliced (optional)*

OR

Dried herb bouquet garni: *1 tsp. parsley, ¹/₄ tsp. thyme, ¹/₄ tsp. basil, ¹/₄ tsp. tarragon, ¹/₈ tsp. marjoram*

Combine all ingredients except bouquet garni in large Dutch oven or stockpot. Bring to boil. Add bouquet garni. (If making a dried herb bouquet garni, place herbs in a double layer of cheesecloth; tie securely.) Reduce heat to low. Cover partially and cook about 5 hours, skimming foam from surface every hour. Add additional boiling water if liquid evaporates too quickly. Strain stock into large pan or bowl and let stand 15 minutes. Carefully skim fat, then strain stock through cheesecloth into another bowl. Refrigerate stock until fat congeals on surface. Skim off fat.

Storing: Stock can be stored in refrigerator up to one week. If it is to be frozen, it can be boiled down to concentrate the strength and reduce its volume. It may be placed in convenient-size containers (such as ice cube trays) and frozen up to 4 months. If you use ice cube trays, remove cubes once they have solidified and store in tightly covered container in freezer.

Note: Ready-to-use canned stocks contain approximately 775 mg. sodium per cup vs. 8 mg. sodium per cup in this version.

* © American Heart Association, reprinted with permission of American Heart Association.
† A whole chicken can be used to make this stock. After simmering about 1 hour, however, the chicken should be removed from the broth. Remove the large pieces of meat from the bones, and return the bones to the broth to continue simmering. The reserved chicken meat can be used for salads, casseroles, sandwiches, etc.

SALT-FREE BEEF STOCK*

YIELD: 1½ to 2 quarts
APPROX. CAL./SERV.: 262

4 lbs. beef or veal bones	*6 sprigs parsley*
1 large onion, cut into 8 wedges	*2 whole cloves*
3 carrots, coarsely chopped	*1 bay leaf*
4 cloves garlic, halved	*1 tsp. thyme*
3 qts. (12 cups) water	*½ tsp. celery seeds*
6 peppercorns, crushed	

Place bones in a roasting pan and brown in a 400° F. oven for 30 minutes. Add onion, carrots, and garlic; continue browning for an additional 30 minutes. Transfer browned bones and vegetables to a large Dutch oven or stockpot. Add remaining ingredients. Bring to a boil. Reduce heat, cover partially, and simmer slowly for about 5 hours, skimming foam from surface occasionally. Strain stock into a large pan or bowl, using several layers of cheesecloth in a colander or large sieve. Cool to room temperature and refrigerate. When ready to use, skim off congealed fat from surface and discard before reheating.

Storing: Stock can be stored in a refrigerator up to one week. If it is to be frozen, it can be boiled down to concentrate the strength and reduce its volume. It may be placed in convenient-size containers (such as ice cube trays) and frozen up to 4 months. If you use ice cube trays, remove cubes once they have solidified, and store in tightly covered container in freezer.

* © American Heart Association, reprinted with permission of American Heart Association.

BAKING

Most commercial baked goods are loaded with hidden sodium. Home baking allows patients to cut down on or eliminate salt, but ingredients and recipes should be chosen carefully. Baking soda and baking powder both contain sodium, as does self-rising flour, since it has one or the other of these already added. For most people, yeast breads and rolls do not present a problem, if they choose a recipe that is low in salt. The small amount of salt that is included in these recipes helps control action of the yeast, which tends to produce a coarse-textured bread if it rises too quickly. Nevertheless, *Craig Claiborne's Gourmet Diet* cookbook has excellent recipes for French bread and whole wheat French bread made without a grain of salt.

In recipes that call for baking soda (sodium bicarbonate), potassium bicarbonate, often available in health food stores, can be substituted in equal amounts. Low-sodium baking powder is also available and it is best to use commercially prepared brands that are sold in small quantities. The low-sodium baking powder purchased in a drugstore is likely to be made up in quantities far too large and expensive to be practical or effective, since it is an unstable product that does not have a long shelf life. The following recipe for homemade baking powder may be used instead:

LOW-SODIUM BAKING POWDER

Cornstarch	56 grams	Potassium bicarbonate	79.5	grams
Tartaric acid	15 grams	Potassium bitartrate	112.25	grams

YIELD: 1½ cups (Recipe may be cut in half)

To substitute for regular baking powder, use 1½ times the amount called for in the recipe. Store in an airtight container and use within six months.

EATING AWAY FROM HOME

Eating out is more manageable than most people imagine, but advance planning is advisable. Restaurants should be chosen carefully to be sure that their menu is varied enough and their staff flexible enough to accommodate the needs of people on a low-salt diet. Happily, restaurants too are realizing that many patrons are health-conscious and that it's good business to offer nutritionally sound choices.

Restaurant owners recommend that patrons call ahead and make their wishes known when making reservations. Many are happy to broil fish, chicken, or beef simply or sauté it in wine or a small amount of unsalted butter, or substitute a dash of lemon juice for salt. Some will add herbs or other seasonings.

If calling ahead is not possible, study the menu for items that are likely to be cooked fresh in individual portions. Avoid dishes that may be prefrozen in individual servings or cooked in large batches, such as stews. Question the waiter carefully about how the dish is prepared and ask if salt, MSG, and soy sauce can be left out. Most restaurants are happy to cooperate, especially if the chef understands that a patron is under doctor's orders to reduce sodium, fat, or other items.

The Cleveland Clinic general guidelines about dining out appear on p. 83.

Bringing lunch to work may be easier and offer more variety than trying to find coffee shops and cafeterias that are able to accommodate a special diet. If there is no refrigerator available for employees, a small Styrofoam cooler or freezer pack may be used. Sandwiches and other luncheon foods can be made in quantity and frozen; they will thaw and come up to room temperature by lunchtime.

On short trips, carrying food may also be preferable to dining out, especially on highways where fast-food restaurants are the only choice. Many hotels will provide a room with a refrigerator for just a few dollars extra. Most airlines will provide a low-sodium meal if it is requested in advance.

TIPS FOR DINING OUT

Appetizers: SELECT fresh fruit or vegetables.

Juice, except tomato juice.

AVOID soups and broths.

Salads: SELECT fresh fruits and vegetables.

AVOID pickles, canned or marinated vegetables, cured meats, seasoned croutons, cheeses, salted seeds. Be conservative with dressings.

Main Courses: SELECT plain foods.

Broiled, grilled, or roasted meats.

SELECT plain vegetables, potatoes, and noodles.

AVOID casseroles, mixed dishes, gravies, and sauces.

When at fast-food restaurants, skip the special sauces, condiments, and cheese.

AVOID salted garnishes such as olives, pickles.

Desserts: SELECT fresh fruits, ices, ice cream, sherbet, gelatin.

7
Exercise in the Treatment of Hypertension

Exercise, along with weight loss, sodium restriction, and other life-style modifications, is an important part of the nondrug treatment of hypertension advocated by Cleveland Clinic physicians. As with all forms of therapy, there are some important "buts" regarding exercise conditioning, especially for patients with cardiovascular disease, including high blood pressure.

In the last twenty-five years, we have come almost full circle in our thinking about exercise for heart patients. Until the late 1950s, most heart patients were advised to "take it easy," not to exert themselves for fear of "provoking" the heart and causing a heart attack. A few leading cardiologists, such as Dr. Samuel I. Levine at Harvard Medical School, had been questioning this attitude, but the public did not become aware of the shift in medical thinking until President Eisenhower suffered his heart attack while still in office. Instead of urging his retirement, his cardiologist, the late Dr. Paul Dudley White, urged him to get back on his feet and to continue as President. Since then, the large majority of cardiologists follow this lead. Experience has shown that most victims of a heart attack do better if they are allowed to move around more, even while in the hospital. Instead of being confined to bed for weeks as in the past, patients are now allowed to get out of bed as soon as their condition stabilizes; to walk around their rooms, up and down the hospital corridors, etc.

Increasingly, exercise conditioning has become an important part of rehabilitation following a heart attack. Now it is not unusual for heart patients to jog; some even enter marathons and other competitive races. Exercise conditioning has also become a part of preventive treatment for high-risk patients with high blood pressure, angina, circulatory problems, and other forms of cardiovascular disease. In fact, jogging and other forms of vigorous exercise are so popular that many people have harbored a mistaken notion that somehow exercise makes them immune from a heart attack.

These misconceptions were sadly put aside with the sudden death of James Fixx, whose books on running had become something of a bible for runners. Mr. Fixx died while jogging alone on a country road in Vermont. What's more, Mr. Fixx was not the only world-class athlete to make headlines because of sudden death while jogging. Philadelphia's John Kelly, brother of the late Princess Grace of Monaco and a world-class athlete since his college days, suffered a similar fate at the age of fifty-seven. And every few weeks, there have been reports of other exercise-related sudden deaths. Understandably, these deaths have raised important questions among both physicians and patients regarding the prudent approach to exercise among people with a high risk for heart attacks.

DESIGNING AN EXERCISE PROGRAM

The human body is built for physical activity, a fact that even Hippocrates recognized. "All parts of the body which have a function," he wrote in 300 B.C., "if used in moderation and exercised in labors in which each is accustomed, thereby become healthy, well developed, and age more slowly; but if unused and left idle, they become liable to disease, defective in growth, and age quickly." Until rather recently in human history, getting enough exercise was not a problem for the vast majority of people. Our ancestors quite literally lived by the sweat of the brow and the fruits of their labor. This began to change with the Industrial Revolution and the introduction of machines to replace human labor. The invention of the automobile and hosts of labor-saving appliances and machines has "freed" most of us of the need to expend any more than minimal physical effort in our jobs or households. In twentieth-century America, we truly can lead a sedentary life.

Unfortunately, our bodies are not designed for a sedentary existence; enter the exercise or fitness boom of the last decade. It did not take long for the word on the benefits of regular exercise to spread: effects such as enhanced feelings of well-being, increased physical endurance and productivity, improved muscle tone, appearance, and obesity control. Almost overnight, it seemed that everyone had taken up jogging, handball, tennis, swimming, or some other vigorous activity. But the impression is misleading; it is estimated that only about 40 percent of all American adults engage in regular vigorous physical activity. Still, this is millions more than a few years ago, and all but a few sedentary holdouts harbor guilt feelings about their inactivity. Most people now think they should exercise, just as most people will agree that they should not smoke, consume excessive alcohol, overeat, or engage in other unhealthful habits. There is little doubt that Americans today are very health conscious, and even those who have unhealthful habits concede that they should change their ways. The problem is, many do not know where to begin.

The first step for the majority of adults, especially people with high blood pressure or any other cardiovascular risk factor, is an exercise prescription from a doctor or other health professional trained in exercise physiology. A number of experts who have studied Mr. Fixx's death and similar episodes contend that these may have been prevented with proper medical guidance.

After Mr. Fixx's death, it was learned that he actually had severe coronary artery disease and several risk factors that had been forgotten or ignored. His father had died of a heart attack at an early age; Mr. Fixx had once been overweight with high blood lipids. When he took up running, he lost the excess weight, stopped smoking, and adopted a healthier life-style. But in the weeks before his death, friends and relatives recalled that he had been bothered by unusual pains in his neck and jaw while running, possible signs that his heart was not getting enough oxygen. Mr. Fixx had not undergone an exercise stress test or a cardiovascular workup. As a number of experts have pointed out: Mr. Fixx was not an exception to the rule that regular vigorous exercise lowers the risk of a heart attack. Instead, his death illustrates an important corollary: Exercise lowers the overall risk of a heart attack but can be fatal in people with undiagnosed heart problems.

Cleveland Clinic physicians recommend that all patients with high blood pressure undergo an exercise tolerance or stress test before beginning an aerobic exercise program. This is in keeping with recommendations of the American Heart Association and American Medical Association's Committee on Physical Fitness and Exercise. An exercise stress test is designed to measure how the heart functions during exercise. Electrodes from the electrocardiographic (EKG or ECG) monitor are attached at specific places on a patient's chest. The patient then exercises, usually on a treadmill or stationary bicycle, at increasing intensity until exhausted or a predetermined heart rate is achieved. The test may be stopped if chest pains, abnormalities on the EKG tracings, or other symptoms occur. Blood pressure and pulse rates are measured before and after the test.

Certain changes in the electrocardiogram tracings may indicate coronary artery disease or disruptions in the heart's normal rhythm and electrical activity. Sometimes these changes occur, even though the heart is normal (a false positive result) and, conversely, some people who in fact have heart disease may test in the normal range (a false negative result). Still, the test is highly useful in identifying people who should undertake an exercise program with special caution and to indicate safe parameters.

Studies have found that even people with severe heart disease can benefit from exercise conditioning. A study by Dr. David Siscovic and his colleagues at the University of North Carolina in Chapel Hill found, for example, that men who exercise regularly (defined as more than 140 minutes of vigorous exercise a week) have a risk of sudden death that is only 40 percent of that of sedentary men (less than twenty minutes of vigorous exercise a week). "Intense physical activity may precipitate primary cardiac arrest (sudden death) in some patients, but habitual participation in such activity is still associated with an overall improvement in risk," Dr. Siscovic concludes. He adds that the incidence of sudden death during exertion probably could be cut if patients heed certain warning signs. These include:

- Any chest discomfort (not necessarily pain; it may take the form of a feeling of heaviness or difficulty in breathing).
- Any discomfort in the abdomen, neck, jaw, or arm.
- Light-headedness or feeling faint.
- Shortness of breath.
- Irregularity of pulse.
- Headache.
- Nausea or vomiting.
- Excessive fatigue.
- Sustained fast pulse after exercising.

Any pain, discomfort, or other warning sign that comes on during or shortly after exercise and disappears after resting for a while is an indication to see a doctor as soon as possible.

HOW MUCH EXERCISE

The degree and intensity of exercise depends upon many factors. Obviously, the work capability of the heart is a major consideration. Age, weight, circulation in the lower extremities, and the condition of the muscles and joints are among the many factors that may limit or determine the type of exercise.

People with hypertension should concentrate on aerobic exercises—activities that exercise the large muscles. Examples of aerobic exercises include walking, jogging, swimming, bicycling, etc. These muscles require extra oxygen to work for any length of time. This means that the heart must pump more blood to the muscles. Normally, the heart pumps about six quarts of blood a minute in an adult nonexercising man who weighs about 150 pounds. This increases to about 25 quarts a minute during peak exercise. To deliver this much blood, the heart has to pump harder and faster; the blood vessels will become more dilated (or open), and some blood will be diverted from the internal organs to the muscles.

As might be expected, systolic blood pressure rises during vigorous exercise, but it returns to its usual level after exercise. Diastolic pressure rises less and may actually fall during exercise. Some studies have found that mild hypertension may be lowered by regular exercise conditioning, especially when it is combined with weight reduction and decreased sodium intake. However, this does not happen in all hypertensive patients, nor is it always a permanent phenomenon. Still, exercise conditioning is considered an important part of the overall treatment of high blood pressure; it is also a sound preventive measure for people whose blood pressures are in the high-normal range.

Exercise conditioning helps reduce several other cardiovascular risk factors. A number of studies have found that regular, vigorous exercise can lower total blood cholesterol. It also increases the ratio of HDL to LDL cholesterol. Exercise is an important part of any weight-control program; overweight runners are very rare. Diabetics who exercise often find they can gain better control over blood glucose and may be able to reduce the amount of insulin needed.

People who exercise regularly are not as likely to smoke as their more sedentary counterparts, and many smokers find that taking up an exercise program is helpful in easing the pangs of stopping smoking. Finally, people who exercise often find they are better able to cope with stress. All of these are important considerations for people with hypertension or any other risk factor that increases their likelihood of a heart attack or other cardiovascular event.

In order for exercise to have a conditioning effect on the cardiovascular system, it must be of sufficient intensity and frequency. To be of sufficient intensity, the heart rate should be increased to a conditioning range, which is defined by the exercise prescription. Each patient may have a different "target range," but in general this is at least 60 percent of the heart's maximum capability. A person's fitness level is usually expressed in terms of METS, or multiples of resting metabolism. Even when you are absolutely still, the body still requires a certain amount of fuel to carry on breathing, circulation, digestion, and other vital functions. This is the basal or resting metabolism. A well-conditioned person can sustain 10 to 15 METS (marathoners or other conditioned athletes may be able to sustain 20 METS). The number of METS a person can sustain is determined by the exercise test. The goal of exercise conditioning is to increase the METS that can be sustained without producing undue fatigue or symptoms of cardiac stress.

In practical terms, an individual exercise prescription specifies a target heart or pulse rate. It works this way: Maximum heart rate is calculated by subtracting a person's age from 220, then adding and subtracting 12 to get the maximum range. For example, a fifty-year-old would have a maximum heart rate of about 170 beats per minute plus or minus 12, or a range of 182 to 158 beats per minute. The cardiovascular conditioning range for a person without heart disease is usually 70 to 80 percent of the maximum rate; for this hypothetical fifty-year-old, 119 to 136 beats a minute. Therefore, for exercise to have a beneficial effect on the cardiovascular system, the exercise will have to be intense enough to raise the heart rate to at least 119 beats per minute. If this fifty-year-old has high blood pressure and signs of coronary disease, the exercise prescription may initially specify a target of 60 to 65 percent of the maximum rate, or a range of 102 to 110 beats per minute.

Obviously, to follow an exercise prescription, the patient must know how to take his or her pulse rate. There are several easy-to-find pulse points on the body: arteries at the wrist, behind the ear, the side of the neck, the temple, etc. A watch with a second hand is also needed. To take a pulse rate, you press a finger against the artery and then count the pulses for 10 seconds. Multiply this by 6 and you have the beats per minute. The pulse rate should be measured before beginning to exercise, at intervals during the workout, and immediately after stopping exercise.

The second part of the exercise prescription specifies the duration and frequency of the workouts. For exercise to have a conditioning effect, it usually must be performed for at least 20 to 30 minutes three or four times a week, preferably on alternating days. At first, an out-of-shape person may be able to exercise for 5 to 10 minutes and at levels below the target heart rate. By gradually increasing the intensity and duration of exercise, most people— even those who have not exercised for years and who have serious heart disease—find that in a few weeks they can exercise for the specified amount of time within their heart target range.

The more vigorous the exercise, the shorter the session can be. Some patients may find they need to exercise for longer periods but at a more leisurely pace. Mrs. Olds, the Cleveland Clinic patient described in chapter 2, tries to swim for an hour a day, five days a week. "I go at a slow pace," she explains, "but I have found that if I swim for an hour, I get as much benefit from the exercise as I would if I did twice as many laps in half the time."

Some patients may find that they start out by walking a half mile in 15 minutes; after a few weeks, they are able to walk a mile in 20 or 25 minutes. Gradually, by increasing their pace, they should be able to attain their goal of, say, 2 miles in 20 minutes with heart rates in the target range for the entire period. But even before reaching that goal, they should notice the benefits of the exercise conditioning.

EFFECTS OF EXERCISE CONDITIONING

One of the first and most obvious benefits of exercise conditioning is increased endurance. After only two or three weeks of regular exercise, most people find they have more endurance for tasks that might have left them feeling tired or out-of-breath before: climbing stairs, walking several blocks to the store, etc. It will also require more effort to increase the pulse rate.

Other, more subtle benefits are also taking place. With exercise conditioning, the cardiovascular system becomes more efficient. The blood increases its oxygen-carrying capacity and the muscles extract more oxygen from the blood. The heart is a muscle and, like any muscle, it becomes stronger with use. Exercise conditioning strengthens the heart and enables it to pump more blood with each beat. This is important because it means that the heart does not have to work as hard to meet the body's need for oxygen. This increased efficiency decreases the resting heart rate and lessens the heart's total workload.

People who undertake exercise conditioning invariably find they not only feel better physically, but also gain renewed emotional well-being. Mrs. Olds described this when she said: "I haven't felt this good in years. I feel I can cope with anything; petty annoyances just don't bother me the way they used to." Blood studies taken during and after exercise have identified some possible biochemical explanations for these feelings of well-being. Exercisers have high levels of endorphins, body chemicals that dull pain and produce a "high" similar to that of morphine. Long-distance runners often describe a "high" that occurs after a few miles; other exercisers maintain that they are addicted to the activity and they feel jittery or out-of-sorts if they cannot exercise. Fortunately, an addiction to exercise does not have the harmful side effects of other addictions, provided, of course, it is done judiciously. There have been reports of some habitual exercisers who have exceeded the dictates of moderation and common sense.

MAINTAINING AN EXERCISE PROGRAM

Very often, people undertake exercise training with great enthusiasm but after a few weeks or months revert to their former sedentary ways. As with other aspects of hypertension treatment, exercise must be sustained on a long-term basis for the benefits to continue. Within a few weeks of stopping exercise, the benefits of conditioning are lost. When this happens, the patient must start all over again to build up endurance and exercise ability.

In designing an exercise program, personal preference and enjoyment are important considerations. Some people may find jogging very boring, but they may enjoy swimming or bicycling. Availability of exercise facilities is another consideration. If a pool is not available, swimming obviously is not a good choice for a regular form of exercise. Many people find they prefer exercising with others; joining a health club or exercise class at the "Y" or community center may be the answer for them. Or simply enlisting a spouse, colleague, or friend for regular workouts may provide the needed companionship and motivation.

Overdoing in the beginning is another common failing. Stressing out-of-condition muscles, tendons, and joints invites orthopedic problems. The knees and feet are particularly vulnerable, especially among people who are overweight. Every exercise session should include stretching exercises to keep the muscles flexible and in good tone. Warm-up and cool-down exercises also are important.

CAUTIONS ON ISOMETRIC EXERCISE

In general, patients with hypertension should avoid weight lifting and other isometric exercises. These activities actually increase blood pressure by constricting blood vessels. Many health clubs feature Nautilus or other weight-training machines. Before using these machines, patients with hypertension should check with their physicians. The same warning applies to other activities that are primarily isometric.

8
Cigarette Smoking and High Blood Pressure

There is little doubt that cigarette smoking increases the risk of a heart attack. This has been demonstrated in study after study conducted in the United States and abroad.

The Framingham Heart Study, one of the most ambitious long-term research projects ever undertaken—almost the entire population of this Boston suburb has been studied since 1948 in an attempt to determine the causes of heart attacks and other diseases—found that men who smoke have a tenfold increase in sudden death from cardiac arrest. Among women smokers, the incidence of sudden death is increased fivefold. Cigarette smoking doubled the risk of a heart attack, heart failure, and stroke. The incidence of occlusive peripheral arterial disease—the blockage of blood flow to the legs or other parts of the body—also was doubled among smokers. In all, Framingham data show that a forty-year-old man who smokes and has high blood pressure is 3.5 times more likely to develop cardiovascular disease than men who do not smoke or have hypertension. Among blacks, hypertension and smoking are the most common cardiovascular risk factors, and both are more prevalent among blacks than the general population.

The latest Surgeon General's Report on Smoking and Health says that 225,000 heart attack deaths in this country each year are, in some way, related to cigarette smoking. Add to this staggering figure the more than 80,000 deaths from lung cancer, 23,000 deaths from other cancers, and 20,000 deaths from emphysema and other chronic lung diseases, and you will quickly see why the Surgeon General says that cigarette smoking is by far the leading cause of preventable deaths among Americans. Worldwide, the number of avoidable deaths caused by smoking is well over one million and rising at an alarming rate.

The combination of cigarette smoking and high blood pressure is particularly lethal. People who both smoke and have hypertension have a much higher risk of heart attacks, sudden death, congestive heart failure, or stroke than people who have either one or the other. This is one reason Cleveland

Clinic physicians and other doctors who treat hypertension make a special effort to help their patients who smoke drop the habit.

Smoking a cigarette has an almost immediate effect on the heart. Blood pressure rises and the heart begins to beat faster almost with the first puff. This means that the heart must work harder than ever to circulate the blood. In addition, the act of smoking lowers the amount of oxygen that is circulating in the blood. Coronary arteries that are already narrowed by fatty deposits or damaged by long-term high blood pressure will have even less oxygen for the heart muscle itself. This makes the heart more vulnerable to cardiac arrhythmias which can lead to sudden death (see Figure 8.1). Smoking also increases vulnerability to angina and heart attacks.

Figure 8.1

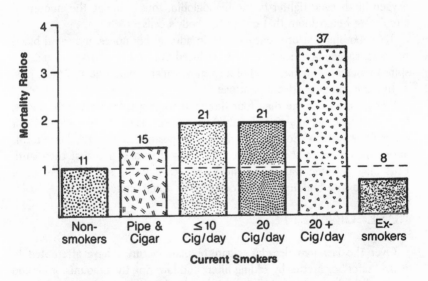

MORTALITY RATIOS AND DEATH RATES*
FOR SUDDEN CORONARY DEATH IN MEN AGED 30-59
BY TYPE OF SMOKING AND NUMBER OF CIGARETTES

*Age Adjusted per 1000
(National Cooperative Pooling Project, A.H.A., 1970)

Some of these adverse effects can be traced to nicotine, the addictive drug in tobacco. Nicotine almost immediately enters the bloodstream when inhaled; it reaches the brain within six seconds of the first puff on a cigarette. Since nicotine is a stimulant, it prompts the adrenal glands to release epinephrine (adrenaline) and norepinephrine, which accounts for the rise in blood pressure and speeded-up heartbeat. Epinephrine stimulates the heart and is also a selective vasopressor—a substance that causes some of the arterioles and other arteries to constrict. Norepinephrine is an even more powerful vasopressor. The narrowing of blood vessels raises blood pressure and reduces the flow of blood to the fingers and toes.

Up to 26 percent of cigarette smoke is made up of carbon monoxide, an odorless gas that is one of the most toxic components of tobacco smoke. When inhaled, it cuts the amount of oxygen in the blood by competing with this vital substance. Carbon monoxide has an affinity for hemoglobin, the part of the red blood cell that carries oxygen, that is more than two hundred times greater than oxygen. When carbon monoxide is inhaled into the lungs while smoking a cigarette, it replaces some of the oxygen that would normally be carried by the hemoglobin to the heart muscle and other parts of the body. The carbon monoxide binds to the hemoglobin, forming a molecule called carboxyhemoglobin. When carboxyhemoglobin is present in the blood, oxygen binds even tighter to the hemoglobin, thus reducing the amount of circulating hemoglobin that enters the body's cells.

This combination of events—a rise in adrenal hormones, increased blood pressure, speeded-up heart rate, and reduced availability of oxygen—all conspire to increase the likelihood of a cardiovascular event: a heart attack, fatal arrhythmia, anginal attack, or stroke.

Since there are more than four thousand components in cigarette smoke, there may be other as yet unidentified adverse effects on the cardiovascular or other body systems. Some researchers have postulated that the body forms antigens to some of these other components of smoke, and that these antigens may in some way injure the blood vessel walls, making them more susceptible to a buildup of fatty deposits, or atherosclerosis.

"SAFE" CIGARETTES

Over the last two decades, cigarette manufacturers have attempted to make "safer" cigarettes by adding filters and lowering the amounts of tar and nicotine in the tobacco. While some research suggests that these low-tar, low-nicotine cigarettes may in some ways reduce the risk of cancer, they do not seem to make any difference to the cardiovascular system. According to the American Heart Association, there is no such thing as a cigarette that is safe for the heart. In fact, some filtered cigarettes may be even more harmful to the heart than regular ones because the unventilated filters increase the amount of carboxyhemoglobin in the blood. Some studies have found a higher death rate from heart attacks among smokers who use unventilated filter cigarettes compared to unfiltered ones.

There is also increasing concern that passive smoking—inhaling other people's tobacco smoke—also has an adverse effect on the heart. Side-stream smoke, which comes from a cigarette left smoldering in an ashtray, has a high concentration of carbon monoxide and inhaling it produces carboxyhemoglobin in the passive smoker. People with heart or lung disease and unborn infants are particularly vulnerable to passive smoking. In fact, the Surgeon General estimates that passive smoking accounts for about five thousand deaths in the United States each year.

STOPPING SMOKING

Of course, the best preventive measure you can take to avoid the cardiovascular hazards of smoking is to never begin. Obviously, for someone who already smokes, this is futile advice. But, as noted in a 1984 update on the Framingham study: "Despite the many and well-demonstrated cardiovascular hazards of cigarette smoking, sixty million Americans continue to smoke or take up the habit. Persons who are predisposed to cardiovascular disease by hypertension, diabetes, or unfavorable lipid [cholesterol and triglyceride] profiles and who elect to continue smoking, place themselves in great and needless jeopardy."

On the brighter side, the Framingham researchers have found that stopping smoking "is also an important aspect of the preventive management of recurrences and premature demise" of people with cardiovascular disease. The American Heart Association has reviewed at least seven studies that show the risk of a fatal heart attack or sudden death is reduced by 20 to 50 percent within five years of stopping smoking.

The Framingham researchers are so impressed with the benefits to be gained from stopping smoking that they write: "Great innovations in the treatment and preventive management of cardiovascular disease have occurred over the past decade. However, there are few drugs or surgical procedures that offer as great potential benefits . . . [to the smoker] as cessation of cigarette smoking."

Of course, most people who smoke already know that it is harmful to their health. There are some people who simply find that the pleasure they derive from smoking outweighs their risks. In other words, they have made their choice; they want to continue smoking no matter what. In a free society, people can make such a choice, even though many of us find it hard to understand.

Fortunately, most people who smoke do want to quit, and large numbers have succeeded. A recent survey of smokers found that 85 percent said they would like to quit smoking. In the twenty years since the first 1964 Surgeon General's report on smoking, some forty million Americans have managed to stop smoking for good. Millions of others have stopped for varying lengths of time. Many of the millions who have "kicked the habit" have been young and middle-aged men; epidemiologists cite this as one of the contributing factors to the decline in cardiovascular deaths in the last twenty years.

Unfortunately, for every smoker who stops, others have taken their place. As a result, there are about as many cigarette smokers today as ever; many of the new smokers are adolescents and women. Indeed, the results of these shifts in types of smokers already are becoming apparent. In 1985, lung cancer surpassed breast cancer as the leading cause of cancer death among women, a factor that the American Cancer Society and National Cancer Institute attribute directly to increased cigarette smoking among women. Some researchers also have noted an increase in heart attacks among women, particularly those who smoke and use oral contraceptives, a combination of factors that increases high blood pressure and cardiovascular risk.

No one has ever claimed that stopping smoking is easy. Nicotine is a powerful addictive substance; a person can become "hooked" on cigarettes after smoking less than a pack. The longer a person smokes, the harder it is to quit. The more cigarettes smoked per day, the more difficult it is to stop. It is also harder for a person who took up smoking at an early age to stop. And for unexplained reasons, it is harder for women to stop smoking than it is for men. Experts worry about the trend among American youngsters to begin smoking at increasingly younger ages. Studies have found that more young women are smoking than ever before and also that most of today's young smokers started in the seventh grade, or between the ages of twelve and thirteen. Researchers at the University of Minnesota found that about a third of all Minneapolis schoolchildren smoked by the end of the seventh grade.

Having said all this, it should be stressed that anyone who wants to stop smoking can, even though it may be difficult. More than ever before, there are sources of help for people who want to become ex-smokers. Increasingly, doctors are taking a more active role in helping their patients stop smoking. Dr. Daniel Horn, Director of the Public Health Service's National Clearinghouse for Smoking and Health, has developed a self-assessment test to help people determine why they smoke (see p. 107). Once a person understands why he or she smokes, it is easier to zero in on the stop-smoking technique that is most likely to succeed.

About 95 percent of all ex-smokers succeeded in quitting on their own. The other 5 percent attended stop-smoking clinics or underwent hypnosis, behavior modification training, or some other specific treatment. About 60 to

70 percent of the ex-smokers had tried to quit previously and then relapsed. On an average, two or more attempts to quit are needed to successfully become an ex-smoker.

Every smoker is different, and what works for one will not necessarily work for someone else. Stopping abruptly or "cold turkey" seems to be the most popular method of quitting, but there are many who succeed by gradually cutting down until they are no longer smoking. In either case, experts recommend drawing up a plan for quitting and then sticking to it.

DRAWING UP A MASTER PLAN FOR QUITTING

Both the American Heart Association and the Public Health Service have drawn up master plans to help people quit smoking. These plans call for the following steps:

• List all the reasons why you want to quit. Every night before going to bed, repeat one of the reasons 10 times. (For starters, see "Reasons for Quitting Smoking," p. 107.)

• Decide positively that you want to quit. Try to avoid negative thoughts about how difficult it might be.

• Develop strong personal reasons in addition to your health and your obligations to others. For example, think of all the time you waste taking cigarette breaks, rushing out to buy a pack, hunting for a light, etc. Think also of the money you will save in the course of a month, a year, five years.

• Set a target date for quitting. Perhaps a special day, your birthday, your anniversary, a holiday. If you smoke heavily at work, plan to quit during your vacation. Make the date sacred and don't let anything change it.

• Begin to condition yourself physically. Start a modest exercise regimen, drink more fluids, get plenty of rest, and avoid fatigue and stressful situations.

• Involve someone else. Bet a friend you can quit on your target date. Put your cigarette money aside every day and forfeit it if you smoke. Ask your spouse or a friend to quit with you.

• Switch brands. Pick a brand that you find distasteful. Change to a brand that is low in tar and nicotine a couple of weeks before your target date. This will help reduce your physical dependence on cigarettes. Keep switching brands; try not to smoke two packs of the same brand in a row.

• Cut down on the number of cigarettes you smoke. Smoke only half of each cigarette. Each day, postpone lighting your first cigarette one hour. Decide you will smoke only during odd or even hours of the day. Decide beforehand how many cigarettes you will smoke and for each additional one you smoke, give a dollar to your favorite charity.

• Don't smoke when you first experience a craving. Wait several minutes and, during this time, change your activity or talk to someone.

• Stop buying cigarettes by the carton. Wait until one pack is empty before buying another one.

• Make cigarettes more difficult to get to. Stop carrying them with you. Lock them up in a drawer or some other place.

• Collect all your cigarette butts in one large glass container as a visual reminder of the filth smoking represents.

• Talk over your strategy with your doctor. When you go to have your blood pressure checked, for example, tell your doctor you have made a firm decision to quit smoking. Let him or her know your stop-smoking date and ask for any additional advice or help. Studies have shown that even five minutes spent discussing stopping smoking with a physician increases the chance of success.

• Before your target date, practice going without cigarettes. Don't think of never smoking again; instead, think in terms of quitting one day at a time.

THE DAY YOU QUIT

• Throw away all cigarettes and matches. Hide lighters and ashtrays.

• Schedule a dentist appointment to have your teeth cleaned to get rid of tobacco stains. Notice how nice your teeth look—and how clean your mouth feels—and resolve to keep them that way.

• Make a list of things you would like to buy for yourself or someone else. Estimate the cost in terms of packs of cigarettes and put the money aside each day to buy these presents.

• Keep very busy on quitting day. Go to the movies (sit in the no-smoking section), exercise, take long walks, go bike riding, visit a friend who does not smoke.

• Buy yourself a special treat or do something special to celebrate.

IMMEDIATELY AFTER QUITTING

• The first few days after you quit, spend as much free time as possible in places where smoking is prohibited, such as libraries, museums, theaters, department stores, churches, etc.

• Drink large quantities of water and fruit juice.

• Avoid alcohol, coffee, and other beverages you associate with cigarette smoking. If you normally smoke a cigarette with your after-dinner coffee, skip both and go for a walk instead.

• If you miss the sensation of having a cigarette in your hand, play with

something else—a pencil, paper clip, rubber band, anything that relieves the feeling of not having something to do with your hands.
• If you miss having something in your mouth, try toothpicks, chewing gum, or a fake cigarette.

AVOID TEMPTATION:

• Temporarily avoid situations you strongly associate with the pleasurable aspects of smoking.
• If you always smoke while driving, take public transportation for a while.
• Develop a clean, fresh, nonsmoking environment around yourself, both at work and at home. Buy a "Thank You for Not Smoking" sign for your office or work area. Don't leave ashtrays around for others to use.
• Until you are confident of your ability to stay off cigarettes, limit your socializing to situations where smoking is prohibited.
• If you must be in a situation where you will be tempted to smoke, try to associate with the nonsmokers there.
• Take a critical look at cigarette ads to better understand the attempts to make individual brands more appealing. The Virginia Slims woman is just as attractive without a cigarette in her hand. The Marlboro Man is just as macho without a cigarette.

FIND NEW HABITS:

• Try to change your habits to make smoking more difficult, impossible, or unnecessary. Try activities such as swimming, jogging, tennis, or handball.
• Wash your hands when you feel an intense desire to smoke.
• Keep your mouth clean and fresh. Brush your teeth more often; use a mouthwash or breath mints.
• Do things that require you to use your hands: crossword puzzles, needle-work, gardening. Treat yourself to a manicure.
• Stretch a lot. If you feel tense or nervous, take a few minutes for progressive relaxation exercises (see p. 115).
• Get plenty of rest.
• Pay extra attention to your appearance. Get your hair styled; buy a new outfit. Bask in the compliments or comments that "You look great (younger, healthier, happier, etc.). What are you doing for yourself?"
• Absorb yourself with activities that are the most meaningful, satisfying, and important to you.
• Add more spontaneity and excitement to your daily routine. Avoid periods of feeling bored.

WHEN YOU GET THE "CRAZIES"

• Keep oral substitutes handy—things like carrots, sunflower seeds (unsalted if you have high blood pressure), apples, celery, sugarless gum, etc.
• Take a shower or bath if possible.
• Learn to relax quickly and deeply. Make yourself limp by visualizing a soothing, pleasing situation and "getting away from it all" for a moment. Concentrate on that peaceful image and nothing else. If this isn't enough, close your door, take the phone off the hook, and take 10 or 15 minutes for relaxation exercises.
• Don't succumb to "One won't hurt." It will. (But if you do, don't consider this an irrevocable sign of failure. You have had a temporary setback, but you still can pick up where you left off.)
• Check with your doctor. He or she is there to offer support and help to get you over these last hurdles.

MARKING PROGRESS:

• Each month, on the anniversary of your quit date, plan a special celebration.
• Periodically, write down new reasons why you are glad you quit and post this list where you will see it often.
• Make up a calendar for the first 90 days. Cross off each day and indicate the money saved by not smoking. Keep a glass jar in a prominent place and put the money saved in it as a reminder of your achievement.
• Set other intermediate target dates and now and then do something with the money you have saved.

PROBLEMS IN QUITTING

Stopping smoking is not easy, but most people who try find it is not as bad as they had anticipated. Almost half of the people who stop smoking are pleasantly surprised to find they suffer very minor, if any, symptoms. Those who do experience withdrawal symptoms find the worst is over in about ten days to two weeks, although a few will continue to crave cigarettes for longer, perhaps several months.

Many of the negative effects are countered by the almost immediate beneficial effects of stopping smoking. Within twelve hours, the body begins to "heal itself." Levels of carbon monoxide and nicotine fall rather rapidly, making it easier to breathe, and there is a renewed feeling of energy and vigor

A FOUR-STEP PROGRAM TO QUIT SMOKING

The Public Health Service, in cooperation with the American Heart Association, American College of Chest Physicians, American Dental Association, and National Association of Community Health Centers, has formulated the following stop-smoking program from the strategies outlined earlier:

STEP ONE

List the positive reasons why you want to quit smoking, and read the list daily. Wrap your cigarette pack with paper and rubber bands. Each time you smoke, write down the time of day, what you are doing, how you feel, and how important that cigarette is to you on a scale of one to five. (See sample "Personal Smoking Record" and "Daily Cigarette Count.")

STEP TWO

Keep reading your list of reasons and add to it if possible. Don't carry matches, and keep your cigarettes some distance away. Each day, try to smoke fewer cigarettes, eliminating those that are least (or most) important (whichever works best).

STEP THREE

Continue with the instructions in Step Two. Don't buy a new pack until you finish the one you're smoking. Change brands twice during the week; each time choose a brand lower in tar and nicotine. Try to stop smoking for 48 hours sometime during this period.

STEP FOUR

Quit smoking entirely. Increase your physical activity. Avoid situations you most closely associate with smoking. Find a substitute for cigarettes. Do deep-breathing exercises whenever you get an urge to smoke.

as more oxygen is delivered to the brain and other body tissues. The senses of smell and taste return within a few days. Usually within a week, the smoker's cough begins to disappear (although it may actually be worse for the first couple of days as the lungs begin to repair themselves). There are also cosmetic effects: the skin will become clearer; the eyes regain lost sparkle; the

PERSONAL SMOKING RECORD

Make up a sheet like this and wrap it around your cigarette pack, using a rubber band. Fill it in after each cigarette.

DATE	TIME	LOCATION	ACTIVITY	PLEASURE RATING*
5/20	7:15 a.m.	Home	Drinking coffee	5
"	8:30 a.m.	Car	Driving to work	4
"	9:15 a.m.	Office	Talking on phone	2
"	10:35 a.m.	Office	Coffee break	4
"	11:15 a.m.	Office	Writing report	1
"	12:30 p.m.	Lunchroom	Drinking coffee	4

* 5, most pleasurable; 1, least pleasurable.

hair loses its tobacco smell; bad breath from smoking disappears. Tobacco stains on the fingers and teeth also disappear with time.

The major problems are related to withdrawal symptoms, from not having nicotine. Irritability, nervousness, anxiety, and an inability to concentrate are the most common symptoms. Some people also have headaches, muscle aches and cramps, visual and sleep disturbances, and a distorted sense of time. The worst period usually occurs about three or four days after stopping, but it normally takes the body about a week to eliminate all nicotine from the bloodstream and body tissues. To help the kidneys flush nicotine from the body, doctors recommend increasing fluid intake to speed the process. Water, fruit juices, weak tea, and seltzer all are good sources of fluid; avoid coffee and other beverages with caffeine, as well as alcohol during this period, especially if you normally smoke when drinking them. Caffeine will increase jittery feelings.

In addition to the physical effects of withdrawal, most people experience psychological symptoms. The psychological effects of breaking a smoking habit are more complex than the physiologic and may persist for weeks or even years. Dr. Horn has found that women are more likely than men to encounter psychological withdrawal problems because women usually smoke for a tranquilizing effect, whereas men tend to smoke for pleasure. People who smoke for psychological reasons report that smoking keeps them on an even emotional keel and helps them suppress feelings of anger and hostility. In a series of interviews with people who had tried but failed to give up smoking, several cited a lack of emotional control. "I started yelling at everyone," one woman said. "Finally, even my husband urged me to start smoking again."

The first two or three months are the most difficult, psychologically speaking. It is during this period that most people resume smoking. Some go underground and become secret smokers, akin to secret drinkers. For example, a person may smoke at the office and deny at home that he or she has resumed the habit. Such actions often lead to feelings of guilt or low self-esteem: "I want to quit but I'm just too weak" is a common refrain. Others will use stress as an excuse to continue smoking. One of the Cleveland Clinic patients described in chapter 2 explained her continued smoking by saying: "I am going through menopause, and I just can't cope with the idea of stopping smoking now. When I get through this, then I'll try to give up smoking."

Researchers have found some validity to this. Many ex-smokers resume the habit during periods of stress. They advise postponing efforts to stop smoking during a stressful period, such as taking a new job or moving.

Many smokers go through a type of mourning when they give up cigarettes. For millions of smokers, cigarettes represent a reliable source of pleasure. Cigarettes may become a love object that needs to be mourned just as much as the loss of a pet or even a loved one. Mourning usually takes at least three months to run its natural course; many ex-smokers report that they intensely "missed" having their cigarettes at least this long.

WEIGHT GAIN

Many smokers cite a fear of gaining weight as an excuse to continue smoking. Studies have found that about 60 percent of men and 50 percent of women gain some weight after stopping, but for most, these gains are rather modest—five to nine pounds. Some of this weight gain is temporary, caused by increased fluid retention during the withdrawal period. Still, if food becomes a substitute for smoking or if care is not taken to watch food intake, twenty or more pounds may be added in a relatively short time. There are several reasons for this. Smoking alters taste sensations; most people who quit smoking are surprised to find how good food tastes. They had actually forgotten what many foods really taste like. Metabolism may change somewhat, reducing somewhat the amount of food the body requires. People who smoke for oral gratification may turn to food instead; they are particularly vulnerable to unwanted weight gain.

Although obesity is a health hazard, particularly for people with high blood pressure, it is not as dangerous as smoking. According to an assessment by the American Cancer Society, "to present the same health hazard as smoking a pack of cigarettes a day, one must be 125 pounds overweight!"

Specific suggestions to avoid weight gain include:

• Have low-calorie foods (unsalted popcorn, fresh vegetables, high-fiber crackers, etc.) on hand for nibbling. (For a list of snacks and their calories see Table 8.1.)
• Don't set a target date for quitting to coincide with a holiday during which there is extra temptation to overeat or overdrink.
• Plan menus carefully and learn to count calories (see chapter 5).
• Increase daily exercise, or join an exercise group.

EXERCISE AS AN ALTERNATIVE TO SMOKING

As noted by Dr. Kenneth Cooper, the father of aerobics, "one of the greatest natural (and legal) 'highs' that one can experience is the sensation of a healthy body in motion." Many ex-smokers concede that they probably could not have stopped smoking if it had not been for exercise. Taking up jogging, brisk walking, cycling, or any other aerobic exercise is a healthful alternative to smoking. In addition, exercise also promotes weight loss and helps lower mild hypertension. (See chapter 7.)

STOP-SMOKING GROUPS

Some people find it impossible to stop smoking on their own. Many have been helped by organizations designed to help people quit smoking. Nonprofit groups like the American Heart Association, American Cancer Society, and the Seventh-Day Adventists give out free information and hold small-group stop-smoking clinics. Smokenders, Smoke Watchers, and other commercial programs also have a high success rate and the money spent to join is often an extra incentive for success. To get a listing of commercial and other programs in your area, check with your local chapter of the American Heart Association or American Cancer Society. Other sources of information and literature include:

American Heart Association
National Center
7320 Greenville Avenue
Dallas, Tex. 75231
(Distributes stop-smoking literature, including "Calling It Quits.")

American Cancer Society
National Office
4 West 35th Street
New York, N.Y. 10001
(Ask for information about their FreshStart quit-smoking program and their "7-Day Plan to Help You Stop Smoking Cigarettes.")

Office of Cancer Communications
National Cancer Institute
Bethesda, Md. 20205
(Write for their "Helping Smokers Quit Kit" and "Clearing the Air: A Guide
to Quitting Smoking.")

American Lung Association
1740 Broadway
New York, N.Y. 10019
(Write for their "Freedom from Smoking in 20 Days" and "A Lifetime of
Freedom from Smoking" brochures.)

DAILY CIGARETTE COUNT

Heavy smokers may prefer to use this type of timetable for recording their smoking habits.

Instructions: Using this form as a model, draw up and attach with rubber bands a "cigarette count" to your pack of cigarettes. Complete the information each time you smoke a cigarette (those from your own pack or those offered by someone else). Note the time and rate how much each smoke means to you (1 is for a cigarette you feel you can't do without; 2 is less necessary; 3 is one you could really go without). Make any other additional comments about your feelings or the situation. This record helps you understand why and when you smoke.

TIME	NEED	FEELINGS/SITUATION
6 a.m.	_____	_____
6:30	_____	_____
7	_____	_____
7:30	_____	_____
8	_____	_____
8:30	_____	_____
9	_____	_____
9:30	_____	_____
10	_____	_____
10:30	_____	_____

Continued

TIME	NEED	FEELINGS/SITUATION
11	_____	_____
11:30	_____	_____
12 p.m.	_____	_____
12:30	_____	_____
1	_____	_____
1:30	_____	_____
2	_____	_____
2:30	_____	_____
3	_____	_____
3:30	_____	_____
4	_____	_____
4:30	_____	_____
5	_____	_____
5:30	_____	_____
6	_____	_____
6:30	_____	_____
7	_____	_____
7:30	_____	_____
8	_____	_____
8:30	_____	_____
9	_____	_____
9:30	_____	_____
10	_____	_____
10:30	_____	_____
11	_____	_____
11:30	_____	_____
12 a.m.	_____	_____
12:30	_____	_____
1	_____	_____
1:30	_____	_____

REASONS FOR QUITTING SMOKING

1. Add years to your life.
2. Help avoid lung cancer, emphysema, bronchitis, and heart attacks.
3. Give heart and circulatory system a break.
4. Get rid of smoker's hack.
5. Feel more vigorous in sports.
6. Improve stamina.
7. Stop smoke-related head and stomach aches.
8. Regain sense of smell and taste.
9. Have smoke-free rooms and closets.
10. End cigarette breath.
11. Save money.
12. Eliminate stained yellow teeth and fingers.
13. Stop burning holes in clothes or furniture.
14. Get rid of messy ashtrays, ashes on carpets.
15. Set a good example for others.
16. Prove self-control.
17. _____
18. _____
19. _____
20. _____

WHY DO YOU SMOKE? A SELF-ASSESSMENT TEST

Here are some statements made by people to describe what they get out of smoking cigarettes. How often do you feel this way when smoking? Select one number for each statement.

5 = always
4 = frequently
3 = occasionally
2 = seldom
1 = never

A. I smoke cigarettes in order to keep myself from slowing down.

_____

B. Handling a cigarette is part of the enjoyment of smoking.

_____

C. Smoking cigarettes is pleasant and relaxing.   _____
D. I light up a cigarette when I feel angry about something.

_____

E. When I have run out of cigarettes I find it almost unbearable until I can get them.   _____

F. I smoke cigarettes automatically without even being aware of it.

                                                          _____

G. I smoke cigarettes to stimulate me, to perk myself up.   _____

H. Part of the enjoyment of smoking a cigarette comes from the steps I take to light up.   _____

I. I find cigarettes pleasurable.   _____

J. When I feel uncomfortable or upset about something, I light up a cigarette.   _____

K. I am very much aware of the fact when I am not smoking a cigarette.

                                                          _____

L. I light up a cigarette without realizing I still have one burning in the ashtray.   _____

M. I smoke cigarettes to give me a "lift."   _____

N. When I smoke a cigarette, part of the enjoyment is watching the smoke as I exhale.   _____

O. I want a cigarette most when I am comfortable and relaxed.

                                                          _____

P. When I feel "blue" or want to take my mind off cares and worries, I smoke cigarettes.   _____

Q. I get a real gnawing for a cigarette when I haven't smoked for a while.

                                                          _____

R. I've found a cigarette in my mouth and didn't remember putting it there.   _____

HOW TO SCORE:

1. Enter the numbers you have selected for the test questions in the spaces below, putting the number you have selected for question A over line A, for question B over line B, etc.

2. Total the three scores on each line to get your totals. For example, the sum of scores over lines A, G, and M gives you your score on Stimulation, etc. Scores of 11 or above indicate that this factor is an important source of satisfaction for the smoker. Scores of 7 or less are low and probably indicate that this factor does not apply to you. Scores in between are marginal.

_____	+	_____	+	_____	=	_____
(A)		(G)		(M)		Stimulation
_____	+	_____	+	_____	=	_____
(B)		(H)		(N)		Handling

	+		+		=	
(C)		(I)		(O)		Pleasurable Relaxation

	+		+		=	
(D)		(J)		(P)		Crutch: Tension Reduction

	+		+		=	
(E)		(K)		(Q)		Craving: Psychological Addiction

	+		+		=	
(F)		(L)		(R)		Habit

Adapted from "Smoker's Self Test" by Daniel Horn, Ph.D., Director of the National Clearinghouse for Smoking and Health, Public Health Service.

INTERPRETING YOUR SCORE

Each smoker's habit is different, but according to studies by the American Cancer Society, most smokers fit into one or more of the following six smoking types. After completing the accompanying Self-Assessment Test, determine what type of smoker you are. Your reasons for smoking should fall into one or a combination of the following:

• Stimulation (10 percent of smokers). This type of smoker uses cigarettes to wake up in the morning, to keep going during the day, for a quick pickup when energies lag. Many people who smoke for stimulation report that a cigarette helps them think more clearly. To give up smoking, find other sources of stimulation. A brisk walk may help wake up in the morning; do a few simple exercises to counter the urge to smoke.
• Handling (10 percent). The smoker enjoys feeling the cigarette, watching the smoke curl, flicking the ashes, making a production of lighting and waving a cigarette. Substitute a coin, pencil, small rubber ball, piece of jewelry, or some other object you like to feel and play with.
• Pleasurable relaxation (15 percent). These smokers find smoking a genuine pleasure. They enjoy a cigarette after dinner or with a cocktail or to enhance a pleasurable feeling (e.g., after sex). Concentrate on some other pleasure enhancer, such as music you enjoy, instead of smoking.

Note: Smokers who fall into the above three categories usually need a substitute for cigarettes to quit: something else that gives them pleasure to handle, other aids to enhance pleasure, something that is stimulating. Once such a substitute is found, quitting becomes relatively easy.

TABLE 8.1. CALORIES IN POPULAR SNACKS

BEVERAGES	Calories
Carbonated (per 8-ounce glass)	
Cola-type	95
Fruit flavors	
(10–13% sugar)	115
Ginger ale	75
Fruit drinks (per 1/2 cup)	
Apricot nectar	70
Cranberry juice	80
Grape drink	70
Lemonade (frozen)	55
Fruit juices (per 1/2 cup)	
Apple, canned	60
Grape, bottled	85
Grapefruit, canned,	
unsweetened	50
Orange, canned,	
unsweetened	60
Pineapple, canned,	
unsweetened	70
Prune, canned	100
Vegetable juices (per 1/2 cup)	
*Tomato juice	25
*Vegetable juice cocktail	20

Coffee/Tea	
Coffee, black	3–5
w/1 tsp. sugar	18–20
w/1 tsp. cream	13–15
Tea, plain	0–1
w/1 tsp. sugar	10
CANDY/CHIPS/PRETZELS	
Candy (per ounce)	
Gumdrops	100
Hard candy	110
Jelly beans	105
Marshmallows	90
Chips (per cup)	
*Corn chips	230
Popcorn (unsalted)	40
*Potato chips	115
Pretzels	
*Dutch, 1 twisted	60
*Stick, 5 regular	10
CHEESE (per ounce)	
*American, processed	105
Cottage, creamed	30
uncreamed	20
*Swiss, natural	105

CRACKERS

Graham, 2–2½ inches square	55
Matzoh, 6 inches in diameter	80
*Rye	45
*Saltine	50

FRUITS (raw)

Apple, 2¾ inches in diameter (medium)	80
Banana, 6–7 inches (about ⅓ pound)	85
Blueberries, ½ cup	45
Cantaloupe, ½ of a 5-inch melon	80
Cherries (per ½ cup) sour	30
sweet	40
Grapefruit, ½ of 3¾-inch fruit	45
Honeydew melon, 2×7-inch wedge	50
Orange, 2⅝ inches	65
Peach, 2½ inches	40
Pear, 3½×2½ inches	100
Plums, 5 1-inch plums	35
Raisins, ½ cup, packed	240
Strawberries, ½ cup	30
Tangerine, 2⅜ inches	40
Watermelon, 2-pound wedge	110

NUTS (per 2 tablespoons)

Almonds	105
Brazil nuts	115
Cashews	100
Peanuts	105
Pecans, halves	95

VEGETABLES (raw)

Carrots, 7½×1⅛ inches	30
½ cup grated	25
Celery, three 5-inch stalks	10
Pickle, 1	15–20

* High in salt and probably should be avoided by people with hypertension.
Source: Calories and Weight, the USDA Pocket Guide, U.S. Department of Agriculture, Agriculture Research Service.

• Crutch/Tension Reduction (30 percent). These smokers use cigarettes for a tranquilizing or calming effect during periods of stress, discomfort, or pressure. Cigarettes are used to cope with problems; success in stopping usually involves learning how to manage the problem situations. A stress management course or behavior modification training may be helpful.

• Craving/Psychological Addiction (25 percent). These smokers are dependent on cigarettes; they usually start craving another cigarette as soon as one is put out. Quitting "cold turkey" is the best stop-smoking method; once the withdrawal symptoms have stopped, the worst is over. Enlist as much help from others as possible.

• Habit (10 percent). These smokers often light a cigarette almost as an automatic reflex; often they don't even realize they have done so. They get little pleasure out of smoking; they do it simply out of habit. Stopping usually involves an increased awareness of their pattern of smoking. Throwing away cigarettes or keeping them in a locked drawer will help. Before lighting up a cigarette, make a conscious effort to ask, "Why do I need this cigarette? Do I really want to smoke now?" Very often, the answer is "no" or "not especially," and in such situations it is easy to forgo smoking.

Adapted from "7-Day Plan to Help You Stop Smoking Cigarettes," © American Cancer Society, 1978.

9
Stress and Hypertension

Many misconceptions abound regarding hypertension; one of the most popular is that the disease is somehow caused by stress or tension. For example, many people still cling to the belief that a hypertensive is automatically someone who is tense, uptight, anxious, or under a lot of pressure. Although many hypertensives fit this description, many others are calm, easygoing, under very little pressure. The fact is, stress may well be a factor in some essential hypertension, but the mechanisms by which it may raise blood pressure are unknown. Also, stress reduction has not been a very effective treatment of hypertension. Still, there is considerable scientific interest in—and debate over—the possible relationship between stress and hypertension as more is learned about the role of the central nervous system in the development of a wide range of diseases.

HYPER-RESPONDERS AND CARDIOVASCULAR DISEASE

Stress is often equated with the pressures of modern society; in reality, it has always been a fact of life. Our prehistoric ancestors faced a host of daily stresses: where to find food, shelter, protection from all sorts of dangers. Through time, the nature of the stresses may have changed, but our bodies respond to them today in much the same manner as in past ages.

In general, stress is defined as a state of being that requires some sort of response or adaptation. It is associated with an automatic "fight or flight" response—a normal, often instantaneous reaction to a perceived danger. For example, a man sees a car bearing down on him as he is crossing the street and he immediately jumps out of its path without even thinking. He later realizes that his heart is pounding and that he managed to move at a considerable speed despite the fact that he recently hurt his knee and has hardly been able to walk, let alone run, at top speed. Stories abound of people who have suddenly acquired almost superhuman strength in the face of imminent danger.

These various responses all are part of the "fight or flight" response. The instant danger is perceived and sets in motion a set of responses in which the adrenal glands almost instantly release the stress hormones—epinephrine (commonly referred to as adrenaline), which speeds up the heart; norepinephrine, which raises blood pressure by constricting the arterioles; and steroid hormones, which increase blood volume and alter metabolism, among other functions. All of this is intended to protect the person, to provide the extra energy that is needed to fight off danger or to flee from it.

Not everyone responds to stress in the same way. Some people exhibit a "fight or flight" response to the slightest provocation or in situations that most of us do not consider a threat. Depending upon the degree of the response, these people are often referred to as hyper-responders. Many people with Type A personalities, characterized by excessive assertiveness, ambition, feelings of hostility, impulsiveness, and time-consciousness, are hyper-responders. Some studies have found that these people also are more likely to have labile hypertension. For example, when their blood pressure is measured at work or in a physician's office, it may consistently be high, but when measured at home or in other settings, it will be normal.

The role of behavior in the development of heart disease is unclear. A number of studies, most notably several by Drs. Ray Rosenman and Meyer Friedman of San Francisco, have identified Type A behavior as increasing the risk of a heart attack. Others have found that it makes little or no difference. More recently, studies have attempted to identify those components of Type A behavior that may be the most harmful. Analyses of personality profiles of heart patients have shown that people who are hyper-responders, with frequent surges in blood pressure in response to anger or feelings of hostility, have a higher incidence of heart attacks than their calmer counterparts, including Type A's whose behavior is not as dominated by hostility. One theory holds that the frequent surges of stress hormones and overstimulation of the sympathetic nervous system may lead to chronic hypertension and may also be involved in the development of atherosclerosis.

According to the Cleveland Clinic's Dr. Tarazi, "We sometimes find people who have been diagnosed as having primary hypertension based on several blood pressure measurements taken in a physician's office. But when their blood pressure is monitored at home, we find that it is normal. Most physicians would agree that it probably is not necessary to initiate antihypertensive drug therapy in these patients if their blood pressures are actually normal most of the time. But we do not know what added risk faces these labile hypertensives. Certainly, they should be monitored periodically, perhaps even undergo a twenty-four-hour automatic blood pressure monitoring to get a better idea of what their pressure is over a longer period of time."

In such a test, the patient is hooked up to a blood pressure cuff that automatically inflates and measures the pressure every few minutes. The measurements are recorded on a tape, similar to the tape made by a twenty-four-hour EKG (Holter) monitor. Since these tests tend to be expensive, in the range of $150 to $200, they are not recommended except in special circumstances.

RELAXATION THERAPY

In recent years, relaxation therapy has been studied as a possible treatment for some hypertensive patients. Techniques may include biofeedback training, in which patients consciously attempt to lower their blood pressure and heart rate; hypnosis; meditation, such as yoga; various relaxation exercises; and behavior modification aimed at minimizing some of the adverse effects of Type A behavior.

"Some studies have found modest reductions in blood pressure," Dr. Gifford observes, "but for the most part, these reductions are temporary and are not reliable or predictable enough to be considered an effective treatment for hypertension." However, some may well be useful adjuncts to other forms of therapy.

Many people find that exercise is a good way of dealing with stress. Others may prefer a combination of vigorous exercise and relaxation techniques. The following progressive relaxation exercises are a modification of a series developed by researchers at Harvard University in the 1930s and later updated by Dr. Herbert Benson of Harvard as part of a nondrug program for hypertensive patients.

PROGRESSIVE MUSCLE RELAXATION EXERCISES

The following progressive muscle relaxation exercises are recommended to promote relaxation during moments of stress or tension. The basic idea is to tense a set of muscles to the point of discomfort, partially relax that tightness, and then fully release the tension. The exercises take about fifteen minutes and should be done while sitting in a comfortable chair, with tight clothing loosened (undo your tie, remove tight belts and shoes, etc.). To get the most benefit, do the exercises with the door closed, phone off the hook, radio silent, and other distractions removed. The idea is to concentrate on the spreading feeling of relaxation and well-being as you progress from head to toe.

STEP ONE—GETTING READY TO RELAX

Take a few deep breaths. Inhale to a count of 3, hold it for a count of 2, and then exhale slowly to a count of 4. Do this at least 5 times before beginning.

STEP TWO—ARMS AND HANDS

Extend your arms in front of you, and tighten both fists as hard as you can. Hold for a count of 10, then relax the fist partway for a count of 5. Finally, let the hands relax completely and take several deep breaths. Before tensing the next group of muscles, softly repeat a relaxing phrase (e.g., "relax" or "peaceful") and envision a serene place, such as a quiet mountain pool or a moonlit beach for 10 or 15 seconds.

Go through the same routine of tensing to the point of discomfort, partial release, and full release with the hands, extending the fingers as far as you can, and then the biceps of the upper arms. Between each set, spend 10 or 15 seconds breathing deeply and envisioning the same quiet scene.

STEP THREE—SHOULDERS AND NECK

The next sets of muscles to be tensed and relaxed are those of the shoulders and neck. First bring your shoulders as far forward as possible, hold for a count of 10, relax somewhat for a count of 5 and then relax completely. Don't forget to breathe deeply and envision your serene place between each muscle set. Next, raise your shoulders as high as possible, hold for a count of 10, relax halfway for a count of 5, then return to a relaxed, normal position. The neck is next; first tip your head back as far as you can, going through the steps of tensing, partial and then full release, followed by deep breathing and serene thoughts. Then push your head forward, tucking your chin down toward your chest, and repeat the usual sequence from tension through complete relaxation.

STEP FOUR—FACE AND MOUTH

Start with the eyebrows. Raise them as high as you can with your eyes wide open. Go through the usual cycle, then close your eyes and squint as hard as you can. Open your mouth as wide as you can; follow this by a set with the tongue pressed hard against the roof of the mouth. At the end of these exercises, take a minute to sit quietly with your eyes closed and concentrate on the relaxed feeling of your upper body and your serene scene.

STEP FIVE—ABDOMEN AND BUTTOCKS

Suck in your stomach muscles as hard as you can, and go through the tension-relaxation cycle. Next, squeeze your buttocks together and go through the cycle.

STEP SIX—LEGS AND FEET

Extend your legs in front of you, raising them 4 or 5 inches off the floor. Point the toes upward, tense the muscles, and go through the cycle. Then curl your toes under as hard as you can.

STEP SEVEN—TOTAL BODY RELAXATION

You have now tensed and relaxed all the major muscle groups from head to toe. You should feel pleasantly relaxed; sit quietly for 5 minutes, eyes closed and basking in this feeling. Continue to envision your quiet scene and breathe deeply and slowly. Finally, open your eyes and stretch. You should feel relaxed but with a renewed sense of energy and well-being. Most people find that 15 minutes spent doing these progressive relaxation exercises is more restful than a 30-minute nap. If these exercises are performed when you are most tense and when energy is flagging, say in midafternoon, you should feel refreshed and ready for several more hours of productive work.

10
The Drugs Used to Treat Hypertension

Without a doubt, the greatest advance in the battle against hypertension has been the development of an array of effective drugs that lower blood pressure (see Table 10.1). These are all relatively new medications, introduced in the last thirty-five years. And even as we write this, other new antihypertensive medications are being developed.

Before the 1950s, there was little that doctors could do to effectively treat primary hypertension. There was even less hope for patients with malignant hypertension—a form of the disease that progresses rapidly and, unless reversed, brings death within a few months. At the Cleveland Clinic, Dr. Irvine Page, widely acknowledged as the father of modern antihypertensive therapy, and his colleagues were undertaking their studies on the effects of renin, serotonin, and other body chemicals that raise blood pressure. *Time* magazine, in its October 31, 1955, cover story on Dr. Page, quoted him as saying:

"Hypertension is not a single disease. It may be almost as variable as the many different forms of cancer. Neither can it have a single cause. There are at least eight mechanisms in the body operating to maintain an even blood pressure, and these are all interrelated. The balance of one cannot be upset without upsetting the balance of the others."

But although Dr. Page was at the forefront in hypertension research and treatment, before the 1950s, he still had little he could offer patients in the way of specific treatments. He used kidney extracts to treat malignant hypertension, with varying degrees of success. He also pioneered the use of hypothermia, or fever treatments, again with only moderate success.

For the more common forms of primary hypertension, Dr. Page and his colleagues could little more than recommend "massive doses of moderation." To quote the same 1955 issue of *Time:*

"First, they reassure the patient by explaining what they can do about his disease. Then they advise him to do what he can to avoid fatigue and excitement. He should spend ten hours in bed and take short naps, often. Every extra pound . . . means work for the heart, so reduce. Moderation is also prescribed in smoking and drinking, in exercise and sexual activity."

At that time, severe salt restriction also was used to treat high blood pressure, but, again, with only moderate success. At Duke University Medical Center, Dr. Walter Kempner developed the rice diet that still bears his name. It cut salt consumption to one tenth of a teaspoon a day, and it did lower high blood pressure in a large number of patients. This in itself was lifesaving in an era when there were no effective antihypertensive drugs. But for the less life-threatening forms of mild to moderate hypertension, the diet was so boring and restricted that most patients had difficulty adhering to it outside a hospital setting. Dr. Page noted that while the rice diet was certainly better than nothing, "a mere 25 percent of patients get their blood pressure down to near-normal levels" by following it, probably because most patients simply could not adhere to it on a long-term basis. Dr. Page supported salt restriction, but in the context of a more normal diet than the rice regimen.

THE FIRST ANTIHYPERTENSIVE AGENTS

To realize just how significant antihypertensive drugs have become in the treatment of high blood pressure, one needs only to go back to 1944 and review the circumstances of President Roosevelt's death. As recalled by Dr. Edward Frohlich, a world authority in antihypertensive drugs who began his research career at the Cleveland Clinic and is now head of education, research, and the hypertension section at the Ochsner Clinic: "FDR had severe hypertension and the only means available then for his treatment was phenobarbital. Initially, there had been some concept that the brain was involved in the elevation of blood pressure, and phenobarbital was the only substance we had that reduced activity in the brain. Now we know that this serves only as a placebo." President Roosevelt died of hypertension at the relatively young age of sixty-three.

In 1951, the outlook for patients with hypertension began to change dramatically with the administration of the first effective antihypertensive drug at the Cleveland Clinic. The patient was a fifty-year-old soft drink manufacturer whose blood pressure was 230/146. He had an enlarged and failing heart and suffered from breathlessness, weakness, and edema. Dr. Page and his colleagues had been studying hydralazine, a vasodilator drug, a class of medications that relaxes the smooth muscles in the arteries, and they decided to administer it to this patient.

Hydralazine acts very quickly. Within fifteen minutes after an intravenous injection of the drug, it begins to lower blood pressure. In a few hours the patient's blood pressure dropped, and over the next few months his other problems began to subside. Eventually, he was able to return to work and again lead a reasonably normal life, even though his heart remained enlarged.

Hydralazine is still used in treating high blood pressure, but it is no longer a first-choice drug. Its introduction at the Cleveland Clinic was quickly followed by the introduction of two other classes of drugs that lower blood pressure: hexamethonium, a drug that blocks ganglionic nerve impulses and lowers blood pressure by dilating the arterioles; and reserpine, a drug derived from the root of an Indian plant, rauwolfia. Reserpine lowers blood pressure by inhibiting activity of the sympathetic nervous system, which in turn lowers vascular resistance, reduces the heart rate and the output of blood from the heart.

Although the introduction of these drugs represented a major breakthrough in the treatment of hypertension, they were not without problems. Hydralazine can cause headaches and tachycardia (rapid heartbeat) and it is not recommended for patients with coronary artery disease or congestive heart failure. It also can cause gastrointestinal upsets, flushing, difficulty in breathing upon exertion, rashes and, in rare instances, nerve and blood problems. Hexamethonium and related drugs cause postural hypotension, which is a marked drop in blood pressure and fainting or lightheadedness upon standing. This is an obvious problem for patients who are not bedridden, and the drugs have largely been replaced by other more effective drugs with fewer side effects. Reserpine is still used but usually in combination with other drugs. Taken alone, reserpine is not potent enough to lower high blood pressures. The drug also has a number of potential side effects, including depression, lethargy, nightmares, nasal congestion, bradycardia (slow heartbeat), and diarrhea. It also can cause a buildup of sodium and body fluid. (For more on the side effects of antihypertensive drugs, see Table 10.2, "Adverse Drug Effects," pp. 133–37.)

THE DIURETICS

In 1958, chlorothiazide was introduced, and again the treatment of hypertension took a giant step forward. Chlorothiazide is the prototype of the thiazide diuretics—a group of drugs that lower blood pressure by increasing the kidney's excretion of sodium and water. These drugs are particularly useful for patients whose high blood pressure is related to increased blood volume and who have problems with accumulation of body fluid. But they seem to work in most patients with mild to moderate hypertension. In fact, studies at the Cleveland Clinic and elsewhere have found that two thirds of all patients with mild to moderate hypertension can be adequately treated with a thiazide diuretic alone. In explaining why he prefers these drugs as the initial antihypertensive agents, Dr. Gifford notes that they are generally well tolerated and that a single low dose of 12.5 milligrams a day is often sufficient. They are also less costly than most other antihypertensive drugs.

A low dose also minimizes the most common side effects of these drugs, which include metabolic problems (rises in uric acid, blood sugar, cholesterol, and triglyceride and reduction in potassium) and sexual dysfunction in men. Since thiazides promote the excretion of potassium as well as sodium and chloride, their prolonged use may result in hypokalemia, a potentially dangerous deficiency of potassium. Dr. Gifford notes that these problems usually can be avoided if the daily dosage of hydrochlorothiazide is less than 50 milligrams. Even so, patients on thiazide diuretics should have their potassium levels measured regularly. Potassium loss may be increased by episodes of diarrhea or vomiting. Potassium is essential for the proper function of muscles, including the heart. If potassium levels fall too low, a potassium supplement may be prescribed.

Since 1958, a number of other potent diuretic drugs have been developed. All diuretics promote the excretion of sodium and fluid, but they have different sites of action. The loop diuretics, which include furosemide and ethacrynic acid, are so named because they work in the part of the kidney known as the loop of Henle. They are more potent than the thiazides, and are usually reserved for patients whose blood pressure is not adequately lowered by the thiazides or who have impaired kidney function or a buildup of fluid in the lungs and heart. Loop diuretics also can deplete the body of potassium, even more rapidly than the thiazides. They also can cause a buildup of uric acid, which may result in attacks of gout.

Still another class of diuretics is the potassium-sparing agents: amiloride, spironolactone, and triamterene. These drugs work in the exchange sites of the kidney tubules, enabling them to increase sodium excretion while sparing the potassium. Care must be taken, however, to prevent hyperkalemia, an excess of potassium, which may occur in patients with kidney failure. They are often prescribed along with a thiazide or a loop diuretic, which minimizes the potassium excretion and other problems and at the same time increases their effectiveness against edema. Spironolactone may cause gynecomastia, an abnormal breast enlargement in men. As with all diuretics, these drugs may cause sexual problems in men.

Since their introduction in the late 1950s and early 1960s, diuretics have been the mainstay antihypertensive drugs. In the last year or two, however, their long-term safety has been questioned by several experts. These critics of diuretic therapy cite results from the long-term Multiple Risk Factor Intervention Trial (MRFIT), a study designed to determine the effects of reducing risk factors on deaths from heart attacks. When death rates among the various groups of MRFIT participants were compared, it was found that a subset of high-risk hypertensive men with abnormal resting EKGs had a higher-than-expected death rate. The subset had been divided into two groups: one designated as special intervention (SI) and the usual care (UC). Both groups had received diuretics, but the special intervention group had been given higher dosages. Dr. Gifford notes that "many of these excess deaths were sudden and unexpected, suggesting arrhythmias perhaps from diuretic-induced hypokalemia, although this has never been proved." He also stresses that among men who had abnormal exercise EKGs the mortality rate was lower in the special intervention group than the usual care subset. Also, other studies involving long-term users of diuretics have failed to document an increased risk of death. In fact, Dr. Gifford stresses that all of the studies which have found a reduction in cardiovascular illness and deaths have used a diuretic as the first-choice drug, and only MRFIT has raised a question about their safety. "All drugs carry some risk, but I have no doubt that there is more risk involved in untreated hypertension than there is in treating it with diuretics."

BETA-ADRENERGIC BLOCKERS

These drugs, commonly referred to as beta blockers, were first introduced in the United States about twenty years ago for the treatment of angina. Propranolol was the first of the beta blockers to be approved by the Food and Drug Administration; since then, a half dozen others have been introduced.

Beta blockers act by inhibiting responses of the beta receptors in the autonomic nervous system. This has numerous effects, particularly upon the heart. Propranolol, which is considered the prototype beta blocker, reduces the oxygen demand of the heart muscle, which slows the heart rate and reduces the amount of blood pumped out. It was first used to treat angina, the chest pains that result when the heart muscle is not getting enough blood. It was soon discovered that the drug also lowered blood pressure. There is decreased blood flow to all body tissues except the brain.

About half of all patients with mild hypertension can be treated with beta blockers alone. These drugs are particularly useful for patients who have coronary artery disease and episodes of angina or cardiac arrhythmias in addition to high blood pressure. Studies have shown that patients given a beta blocker following a heart attack are less likely to suffer a subsequent heart attack or sudden death. Since they do not affect levels of uric acid, they are useful for hypertensive patients who also suffer from gout. These drugs should not be taken by patients with congestive heart failure and should be used along with a diuretic by patients with edema. They are contraindicated for patients with bradycardia (slow heartbeat), asthma, or chronic lung disease, since they may worsen these conditions. Beta blockers tend to increase blood cholesterol and triglycerides and to lower the protective HDL cholesterol. But these changes usually are not enough to contraindicate their use in patients who have coronary disease since their protective effect probably exceeds the adverse effect of a modest rise in cholesterol.

Most patients tolerate beta blockers well. About 5 percent of patients complain of unusual tiredness or lethargy while taking beta blockers. Some men experience impotence or loss of sexual desire. Other less common adverse reactions include depression, mood changes, nightmares or vivid dreams, itching or other skin irritations, gastrointestinal upsets, and respiratory problems.

Individual people may react differently to different beta blockers. For example, if one causes impotence or some other undesirable side effect, the problem may be solved by lowering the dosage or switching to another beta blocker.

Care must be taken not to abruptly stop a beta blocker since this may result in a worsening of angina or even precipitate a heart attack. When going off a beta blocker, the dosage should gradually be decreased over a one- to two-week period, with special attention paid to any symptoms that may indicate a worsening heart problem.

ALPHA ADRENERGIC BLOCKING AGENTS

Like beta blockers, these drugs also work through the autonomic nervous system by blocking the alpha receptors. They lower blood pressure by dilating the arterioles and are generally used in combination with other antihypertensive drugs. Alpha blockers also interfere with the action of stress hormones.

Prazosin is the major drug in this category; it is less likely to cause tachycardia (rapid heartbeat) than other alpha blockers. But it can cause orthostatic hypotension, especially after the first dose. Patients who are just beginning treatment with prazosin should be careful about standing suddenly, since this may produce a sudden drop in blood pressure and dizziness or fainting. Prazosin is particularly useful for patients who have congestive heart failure or pheochromocytoma, a type of tumor that produces epinephrine and norepinephrine.

CENTRALLY ACTING DRUGS

These drugs lower blood pressure by suppressing the sympathetic nervous system, thereby reducing heart rate, the heart's output of blood, and the resistance of the peripheral blood vessels. Drugs in this category include methyldopa, clonidine, and guanabenz. They are prescribed with a diuretic and are reserved for patients whose blood pressure is not sufficiently lowered with a diuretic alone or by a diuretic and beta blocker.

Drowsiness, dryness of the mouth, and constipation are the most common adverse reactions. Sometimes dizziness or orthostatic hypotension occurs, usually at the beginning of treatment. Some patients, especially those in jobs that demand mental sharpness, also complain about a reduction in their ability to think clearly. Care must be taken not to stop these drugs abruptly; this can cause serious rebound hypertension and a hypertensive crisis due to the sudden release of norepinephrine, a stress hormone.

PERIPHERAL ADRENERGIC ANTAGONISTS

These drugs lower blood pressure by interfering with the release of norepinephrine from sympathetic nerve endings in response to a stimulus. Reserpine, which is derived from the root of the Indian rauwolfia plant, is one of the older antihypertensive agents. Other drugs in this category include guanadrel and guanethidine.

Reserpine is sometimes used alone to treat mild or moderate hypertension, but more often the drug is used along with a thiazide diuretic for patients whose blood pressure is not controlled with a diuretic alone. Guanethidine is a more potent antihypertensive drug and is usually prescribed for patients with severe hypertension that is not controlled by other drug regimens. Its major side effect is orthostatic hypotension, which may result in light-headedness or fainting upon standing up or during exercise. Another drug, guanadrel, is not as potent as guanethidine, but it has similar (though less frequent and less severe) side effects. It is used in treating milder hypertension, usually with a diuretic. Sodium and water retention may occur with drugs in this category if they are not given along with a diuretic. Patients taking reserpine may encounter central nervous system problems, such as lethargy, nightmares, and mental depression; the drug should not be taken by patients who have suffered from depression and it should be discontinued if symptoms of depression occur.

VASODILATORS

These are drugs that dilate or expand the blood vessels, thereby allowing blood to flow through them with less resistance. Hydralazine, the oldest antihypertensive agent, is a vasodilator; other drugs in this category include diazoxide, minoxidil, and nitroprusside. As noted earlier, these drugs have a number of side effects, but they are useful when combined in small doses with other antihypertensive agents to lower blood pressure that is resistant to other treatments. They are also useful in hypertensive emergencies because they act quickly with a dramatic lowering of blood pressure. Minoxidil is one of the most potent of all antihypertensive drugs, but it causes excessive growth of facial and body hair (hirsutism).

CONVERTING ENZYME INHIBITORS

These are among the newest antihypertensive drugs. They lower blood pressure by blocking the enzyme that converts angiotensin I to angiotensin II, one of the body's most potent chemicals that increase blood pressure. Angiotensin is produced in response to the release of renin from the kidney; therefore, these drugs are particularly useful in treating hypertensive patients whose high blood pressure is related to excessive renin activity. Drugs in this category are captopril and enalapril. They are usually prescribed with a diuretic, which increases their effectiveness.

Special care must be taken in giving these drugs to people with kidney disease; kidney failure has occurred in some patients with preexisting loss of kidney function. Other adverse reactions include blood disorders, rashes, hypotension, and a reversible loss of taste.

CALCIUM CHANNEL BLOCKERS

These also are new drugs and are used mostly for angina, particularly the type that occurs while a patient is at rest, and is caused by a spasm of a coronary artery. Calcium channel blockers interfere with the action of calcium on the artery muscles, resulting in a dilation of the blood vessels and a drop in blood pressure. Drugs in this category include verapamil, diltiazem, and nifedipine. They are usually prescribed with a diuretic and their use with a beta blocker is generally avoided. Calcium channel blockers are contradicted for patients who have heart block or other disturbances in their cardiac electrical system. Adverse reactions with calcium channel blockers include headaches, dizziness, palpitations, gastrointestinal disturbances, rashes, and swelling of the lower legs.

INITIATING ANTIHYPERTENSIVE DRUGS

High blood pressure is a disease that can be treated, but as yet we do not have a cure for the most common type, primary hypertension. In most instances, antihypertensive therapy is for life. As stressed in chapter 4, many factors are taken into consideration before prescribing antihypertensive drugs. In addition to the level of blood pressure, factors that should be considered include age, race, family and personal medical backgrounds, weight, and life-style.

In recent years, there has been an increasing tendency to prescribe antihypertensive drugs at lower levels of blood pressure. According to Dr. Gifford, "most authorities now agree that drug treatment is indicated for patients with diastolic blood pressures of 100 mm Hg or higher and for patients with diastolic pressures of 95 to 99 mm Hg if nondrug treatment fails to reduce it to 90 or less after three to six months."

Many doctors also advocate drug treatment for patients whose diastolic pressures are in the 90 to 94 range, while others prefer to take frequent blood pressure readings and initiate treatment if it rises or there is evidence of organ damage. Dr. Gifford and his Cleveland Clinic colleagues usually recommend drugs for these mild hypertensives if six months of nondrug therapy —salt restriction, weight control, and exercise—do not lower the readings to less than 90. "Long-term studies such as the Hypertension Detection and Followup Program have shown conclusively that the mortality rate can be reduced for these patients when drugs are used."

Cleveland Clinic physicians do not advocate antihypertensive drugs for patients in the high-normal range, defined as diastolic blood pressures of 85 to 89 mm Hg. "These patients deserve closer surveillance than persons with lower diastolic blood pressures because they are at intermediate risk," Dr. Gifford explains. "However, nondrug treatment, especially cutting back on sodium and obesity control, as well as exercise, may be advisable for people who have family histories of hypertension and premature cardiovascular disease."

People with mild hypertension who have other major cardiovascular risk factors—high blood cholesterol, cigarette use, obesity, or a family history of early heart attacks—are stronger candidates for drug therapy than people with similar blood pressure readings but no other risk factors. Similarly, drug therapy may be started in a high-risk man in his thirties or forties than in a person over sixty-five or seventy with the same modest elevation in blood pressure. However, Dr. Gifford cautions that the idea that high blood pressure is "normal" in older people has been discounted, and that old age is not a reason to withhold antihypertensive therapy.

There is still disagreement among physicians as to when to begin drug treatment to lower high systolic pressure when the diastolic readings are 90 or less. "More and more doctors are prescribing antihypertensive drugs for patients with systolic pressures of 160 or higher, even when the diastolic readings are 90 or lower," Dr. Gifford observes, "even though no studies have demonstrated that this reduces their risk. I agree with this practice although, in this instance, age plays a role in my decision. If there is no organ damage —e.g., impaired kidneys, enlarged heart, or eye damage—I usually do not prescribe antihypertensive drugs for patients over the age of seventy until the systolic pressure is 170 or higher, provided, of course, that the diastolic pressure is normal."

Dr. Donald Vidt, head of the Cleveland Clinic treatment program for hypertension, emphasizes that the best time to begin antihypertensive drugs is before there is evidence of organ damage. "Mortality is more than three times higher among people who begin treatment after organ damage such as coronary artery disease, heart enlargement, or kidney impairment than among hypertensives without these complications."

But even if there is considerable organ damage, "it is still worthwhile to treat the hypertension aggressively," Dr. Gifford stresses. "Heart attacks, strokes, and other serious cardiovascular events still can be reduced and life prolonged, although not to the same extent that would have been possible if treatment had been started earlier."

THE STEPPED CARE APPROACH

As noted earlier, the goal of antihypertensive therapy is to bring the diastolic blood pressure as near normal as possible without endangering the patient with toxic or intolerable side effects. Studies such as the Hypertension Detection and Followup Program have clearly shown that the Stepped Care Approach, in which there is a definite treatment goal, offers the best chance of avoiding premature death or hypertension-related illness. In recent years, the traditional Stepped Care Approach has been reevaluated and Cleveland Clinic doctors may modify it according to individual circumstances. But the basic framework for therapy is the same as outlined in Table 10.3.

The Stepped Care Approach has been developed over the last two decades and modified as new drugs become available or collective experience has provided new insight into the most effective way to treat high blood pressure.

Cleveland Clinic doctors, many of whom have worked with the Joint National Committee on Detection, Evaluation, and Treatment of High Blood Pressure to formalize the Stepped Care Approach, sometimes modify the recommendations to meet individual patient needs. For example, many favor a half step between Steps 1 and 2; instead of going to the full dose of the Step 1 drug, they have found that some patients may benefit from a low dose of a thiazide to which a low dose of a beta blocker is added, rather than proceeding to the full dose of the diuretic before adding another drug.

SPECIAL CONSIDERATIONS

Dr. Gifford and his colleagues generally favor a thiazide diuretic as the initial Step 1 drug, especially in black patients (who seem to do better on these drugs than on beta blockers) or patients with circulatory or respiratory problems. A beta blocker may be favored for patients with angina or those who have had a heart attack, as well as for patients with gout or for those who are susceptible to migraine headaches or other conditions that may be treated by these drugs.

Since short-term diuretic therapy causes an increase in blood cholesterol and triglycerides, patients using these drugs are urged to eat a diet that is low in red meats, eggs, whole milk, butter, cheese, and other saturated fats. Unless a potassium-sparing diuretic is prescribed, patients should have their serum potassium levels measured periodically. Patients troubled by gout may be switched to a beta blocker, or drugs to prevent a buildup of uric acid—the blood chemical that causes the painful attacks—may be prescribed.

When beginning antihypertensive therapy, a patient should see his or her physician frequently, sometimes every week or two. This allows a doctor to monitor the effectiveness of the drugs and to adjust dosages, check on adverse reactions, and find out if there are any other problems. Often, patients are reluctant to bring up certain side effects, or they think they must suffer in order for the drugs to work. Still others drop out of treatment, especially if the drugs make them feel sicker than before they started therapy. In reality, most side effects can be controlled or minimized, by either adjusting the dosage or switching drugs. Others are temporary and will cease once the body becomes adjusted to the drug.

Problems of sexual dysfunction are common examples of side effects encountered by men taking antihypertensive drugs. Many men either are reluctant to talk to their doctors about diminished sexual desire or impotence, or do not associate these problems with the antihypertensive drugs. Others will simply drop out of treatment, preferring to take their chances on living with hypertension rather than sacrificing this aspect of their lives. Although there are many causes of sexual dysfunction, it is well known that some antihypertensive regimens cause sexual problems. Very often, these can be minimized or overcome by adjusting the treatment.

At the beginning, many patients have problems remembering to take their drugs or they unwittingly take the wrong dosages. Many antihypertensive medications can now be taken once or twice a day; there also are combinations of antihypertensive drugs that reduce the number of pills a patient must take in a multidrug regimen. These combination pills also tend to be less expensive. However, many doctors prefer the flexibility of fine-tuning doses with separate pills. Patients should make sure they fully understand their regimen before leaving the doctor's office. Cleveland Clinic physicians write out instructions in addition to explaining the specific regimen to a patient. (For more on the dosages for antihypertensive agents, see Table 10.3 on p. 138.)

Hypertension is a lifelong disease and it is important that the patient and doctor form a comfortable working partnership in managing the disease. If a patient is having problems following a regimen, enlisting the help of a family member or close friend may help. "We've found that some patients are more apt to remember to take their drugs if a spouse or other family member helps remind them," Dr. Vidt says. "Others find they remember better if they learn to associate taking their medication with some other daily activity. For example, if drugs are to be taken in the morning and evening, patients can make it a point to take them at the same time as they brush their teeth. Some men keep their antihypertensive medication with their shaving equipment to remind them to take their morning dosage when they shave."

Mrs. Olds, the Cleveland Clinic patient described in chapter 2, has been on as many as thirty pills a day. When asked how she managed to keep that many pills straight, she said: "I started by keeping a chart that told me exactly what pill I was to take when. I made sure that the pills were kept in order in their own clearly labeled bottles. I would check off each pill on the chart as I took it, and at the end of the day I would review the chart to make sure I had not missed any."

Now Mrs. Olds is on a simpler regimen which involves four different drugs plus insulin injections for her diabetes. "By now, taking my medication is a part of my daily regimen and I know that when I brush my teeth in the morning, I take two pills plus my insulin. At lunchtime I take more pills and I take the last ones with my evening insulin."

Mr. Rhodes, who travels frequently, has learned to pack his pills first in a carry-on bag. "I made the mistake once of packing my pills in a suitcase that I checked through to my destination. Of course, that was the bag that was

TABLE 10.1. ANTIHYPERTENSIVE AGENTS*

	Dosage Range† (mg/day) Initial Maximum‡
DIURETICS	
Thiazides and related sulfonamide diuretics	
Bendroflumethiazide (Naturetin)	2.5 – 5
Benzthiazide (Exna, Hydrex)	25.0 – 50
Chlorothiazide sodium (Diuril)	250.0 – 500
Chlorthalidone (Hygroton, Thalitone)	25.0 – 50
Cyclothiazide (Anhydron, Fluidil)	1.0 – 2
Hydrochlorothiazide (Esidrix, HydroDIURIL, Oretic)	25.0 – 50
Hydroflumethiazide (Diucardin, Saluron)	25.0 – 50
Indapamide (Lozol)	2.5 – 5
Methyclothiazide (Aquatensen, Enduron)	2.5 – 5
Metolazone (Diulo, Zaroxolyn)	2.5 – 5
Polythiazide (Renese)	2.0 – 4
Quinethazone (Hydromox)	50.0 – 100
Trichlormethiazide (Metahydrin, Naqua)	2.0 – 4
Loop diuretics	
Bumetanide** (Bumex)	0.5 – 10††
Ethacrynic acid (Edecrin)	50.0 – 200††
Furosemide (Lasix)	80.0 – 480††
Potassium-sparing agents	
Amiloride hydrochloride (Midamor)	5.0 – 10
Spironolactone (Aldactone)	50.0 – 100
Triamterene (Dyrenium)	50.0 – 100
ADRENERGIC INHIBITORS	
Beta-adrenergic blockers‡‡	
Atenolol (Tenormin)	25.0 – 100
Metoprolol tartrate (Lopressor)	50.0 – 300
Nadolol (Corgard)	20.0 – 120
Oxprenolol hydrochloride (Trasicor)	160.0 – 480
Pindolol (Visken)	20.0 – 60††
Propranolol hydrochloride (Inderal)	40.0 – 480††
Propranolol long-acting (LA Inderal)	80.0 – 480
Timolol maleate (Blocadren)	20.0 – 60††
Central adrenergic inhibitors	
Clonidine hydrochloride (Catapres)	0.2 – 1.2††

	Dosage Range† (mg/day) Initial Maximum‡
Guanabenz acetate (Wytensin)	8.0 – 32††
Methyldopa (Aldomet)	500.0 –2000††
Peripheral adrenergic antagonists	
Guanadrel sulfate (Hylorel)	10.0 – 150††
Guanethidine monosulfate (Ismelim)	10.0 – 300
Rauwolfia alkaloids (Harmonyl, Raudixin)	50.0 – 100
Reserpine (Reserpine)	0.05– 0.25
Alpha-1 adrenergic blocker	
Prazosin hydrochloride (Minipress)	1.0 – 20††
Combined alpha-and-beta adrenergic blocker	
Labetalol hydrochloride (Normodyne, Trandate)	200.0 –1200
VASODILATORS	
Hydralazine hydrochloride (Apresoline)	50.0 – 300††
Minoxidil (Loniten)	5.0 – 100††
ANGIOTENSIN-CONVERTING ENZYME INHIBITORS	
Captopril (Capoten)	37.5 – 150††
Enalapril maleate***	10.0 – 40
SLOW CHANNEL CALCIUM-ENTRY BLOCKING AGENTS	
Diltiazem hydrochloride (Cardizem)	120.0 – 240†††
Nifedipine (Procardia)	30.0 – 180†††
Verapamil hydrochloride (Calan, Isoptin)	240.0 – 480†††

   * All drugs are listed by generic name. If more specific information is desired, consult the *Physicians' Desk Reference*, thirty-ninth edition, 1985.

   † The dosage range may differ slightly from recommended dosage in the *Physicians' Desk Reference* or package insert.

   ‡ The maximum suggested dosage may be exceeded in resistant cases.

  ** These drugs have not been approved for the treatment of high blood pressure by the Food and Drug Administration (FDA).

 †† This drug is usually given in divided doses twice daily.

 ‡‡ Atenolol and metoprolol are cardioselective; oxprenolol and pindolol have partial agonist activity.

*** This drug has not been approved by the FDA.

††† This drug is usually given in divided doses three or four times daily.

lost for two days. I had to call my doctor at the clinic to have him telephone in prescriptions to the pharmacy in my hotel."

Getting pills mixed up is a common mistake, but one that can have serious consequences because it may mean overdosing on a potent medication. Cleveland Clinic doctors instruct patients never to mix pills in a bottle or pillbox. "It's a good idea to keep medications in their original bottles," Dr. Vidt advises. "If a patient does take pills from a bottle to have a supply at the office, for example, make sure they are in a clearly labeled bottle like the original one. Never carry more than one drug in the same container; it's too easy to make a mistake, even if the pills look different."

Some of the drugs used to treat hypertension are expensive and patients on a limited income may have difficulty maintaining long-term therapy. Some patients will try to make the drugs go further by cutting the dosages themselves, or will drop out of treatment altogether. "If a patient is having trouble paying for medication or physician visits, the doctor should be informed," Dr. Vidt stresses. "There are a number of programs to help such patients. In the long run, controlling high blood pressure costs only a fraction of treatment of a stroke, heart attack, or kidney failure."

Many patients need reminders from their doctors regarding follow-up appointments or medication checks. "If a patient fails to make or keep a follow-up appointment, a call from the doctor or nurse will usually suffice," Dr. Vidt says. This tells the patient that the doctor really cares; it also reemphasizes the importance of follow-up.

Usually, antihypertensive therapy is for life. There have been some recent reports of patients who have been able to stop their medication after a few years on the drugs. "In my experience, this is very unusual," Dr. Gifford says. "In almost every instance, the blood pressure will go back up. It may be normal for a few months or even a year, but then it will return to its former high levels, or go even higher. The exceptions might be people who had mild hypertension and who changed their life-styles—they may have lost weight, stopped smoking, cut back on salt consumption, started exercising more— while on the drugs. Such patients may be able to get by on lowered dosages or even no drugs at all. But they are the exceptions rather than the rule."

To summarize, there are now a large number of effective antihypertensive medications, meaning that most people with high blood pressure can be treated effectively. By careful adjustment of dosages or switching drugs, side effects can be eliminated or minimized. Above all, a return to normal blood pressure does not mean that the disease is cured and the drugs can be stopped. Hypertension therapy is a lifelong proposition, and one that has been proved to prolong life.

Table 10.2 ADVERSE DRUG EFFECTS

DRUGS (Brand Name)	Side Effects	Precautions and Special Considerations
DIURETICS **Thiazides and related sulfonamide diuretics** Bendroflumethiazide (Corzide, Naturetin, Rauzide) Benzthiazide (Exna, Hydrex) Chlorothiazide sodium (Diuril) Chlorthalidone (Hygroton, Thalitone) Cyclothiazide (Anhydron, Fluidil) Hydrocholorothiazide (Esidrix, HydroDIURIL, Oretic) Hydroflumethiazide (Diucardin, Saluron) Indapamide (Lozol) Methyclothiazide (Aquatensen, Enduron) Metolazone (Diulo, Zaroxolyn) Polythiazide (Renese) Quinethazone (Hydromox) Trichlormethiazide (Metahydrin, Naqua)	Hypokalemia (potassium depletion), high uric acid (hyperuricemia), high blood sugar, high cholesterol and triglycerides, sexual dysfunction, gastrointestinal upsets, skin rash, sensitivity to sunlight.	May be ineffective in kidney failure. Potassium depletion increases sensitivity to digitalis. High uric acid content may precipitate acute gout.

DRUGS (Brand Name)	Side Effects	Precautions and Special Considerations
Loop diuretics Bumetanide (Bumex)* Ethacrynic acid (Edecrin) Furosemide (Lasix)	Same as for thiazides.	Effective in chronic kidney failure. Potassium depletion and high uric acid dangers same as for thiazide. Hyponatremia (sodium depletion) may occur, especially in the elderly.
Potassium-sparing agents Amiloride hydrochloride (Midamor)	Hyperkalemia (excessive potassium).	Patients with kidney failure more susceptible to hyperkalemia.
	Sexual dysfunction.	
Spironolactone (Aldactone)	Gynecomastia (abnormal breast growth), breast pain, sexual dysfunction	
Triamterene (Dyrenium)	Gastrointestinal disturbances.	
ADRENERGIC ANTAGONISTS **Beta-adrenergic blockers†** Acebutolol (Sectral) Atenolol (Tenormin) Metoprolol (Lopressor) Nadolol (Corgard) Oxprenolol hydrocloride (Trasicor)‡ Pindolol (Visken) Propranolol hydrochloride (Inderal)	Slow heartbeat (bradycardia), fatigue, insomnia, bizarre dreams, sexual dysfunction, high triglyceride count, decreased HDL cholesterol.	Should not be used in patients with asthma, chronic obstructive pulmonary disease (emphysema), congestive heart failure, and certain cardiac electrical disorders. Should be used with caution in patients with diabetes mellitus and circulatory disorders.

DRUGS (Brand Name)	Side Effects	Precautions and Special Considerations
Central-acting adrenergic inhibitors		
Clonidine hydrochloride (Catapres) Guanabenz acetate (Wytensin)	Drowsiness, dry mouth, fatigue, sexual dysfunction.	Rebound hypertension may occur with abrupt discontinuance of drug.
Methyldopa (Aldomet)		May cause liver damage and result in positive direct Coombs test for antibodies directed against red blood cells.
Peripheral-acting adrenergic inhibitors	Sexual dysfunction, nasal congestion.	
Guanadrel sulfate (Hylorel) Guanethidine monosulfate (Esimil)	Orthostatic hypotension (dizziness upon standing up quickly), diarrhea.	Should be used cautiously in elderly patients because of orthostatic hypotension.
Rauwolfia alkaloids (Harmonyl, Raudixin) Reserpine (Reserpine)	Lethargy, nasal congestion, aggravation of peptic ulcer.	Contraindicated for patients with history of mental depression.

Managing Hypertension

DRUGS (Brand Name)	Side Effects	Precautions and Special Considerations
Alpha-1 adrenergic blocker Prazosin hydrochloride (Minipress)	Fainting upon initiation of therapy, orthostatic hypotension, weakness, heart palpitations.	Use cautiously in elderly patients because of orthostatic hypotension.
Combined alpha-and-beta adrenergic blockers Labetalol hydrochloride (Normodyne, Trandate)	Nausea, fatigue, dizziness. Bronchospasm, headache (rare).	Contraindicated for patients with certain cardiac electrical disturbances. Use with caution in patients with cardiac failure, bronchial asthma, emphysema, and diabetes mellitus.
VASODILATORS	Headache, rapid heartbeat (tachycardia), fluid retention.	May precipitate angina in patients with coronary heart disease.
Hydralazine hydrochloride (Apresoline)	Lupus-like symptoms (rare at recommended doses).	Positive results from tests for lupus.
Minoxidil (Loniten)	Excessive hairgrowth (hypertrichosis), ascites (fluid in the abdominal cavity) (rare).	May cause or aggravate excess fluid in the pleural (lung) and pericardial (around the heart) cavities.

DRUGS (Brand Name)	Side Effects	Precautions and Special Considerations
ANGIOTENSIN-CONVERTING ENZYME INHIBITORS Captopril (Capoten) Enalapril maleate*	Skin rash and altered sense of taste (rare at recommended doses).	Can cause kidney failure in patients with renal artery disease on both sides. Neutropenia (shortage of neutrophils, one type of white blood cell) may occur in patients with autoimmune-collagen disorders. Proteinuria (protein in the urine) may occur but is rare at recommended doses.
SLOW CHANNEL CALCIUM-ENTRY BLOCKING AGENTS°	Headache, hypotension, dizziness.	
Diltiazem hydrochloride (Cardizem)	Nausea.	Use with caution in patients with congestive heart failure or certain cardiac electrical disturbances.
Nifedipine (Procardia)	Edema, flushing, nasal congestion, gastrointestinal disturbances, skin rashes.	———
Verapamil hydrochloride (Calan, Isoptin)	Flushing, edema, bradycardia, constipation.	Same as for diltiazem hydrochloride.

° Not yet approved by the FDA for the treatment of hypertension as of June 1985.
† Sudden withdrawal has been reported to be hazardous in patients with heart disease.
‡ Not currently marketed.

TABLE 10.3. STEPPED CARE APPROACH TO ANTIHYPERTENSIVE DRUG THERAPY

STEP 1   Begin with a less than   OR   Begin with a less
         full dose of a thiazide   than full dose of a
         diuretic   beta blocker

Proceed to full dose if necessary or desirable

IF TARGET BLOOD PRESSURE GOAL IS NOT ACHIEVED:

STEP 2   Add a small dose of an   OR   Add a small dose of a
         adrenergic inhibiting   thiazide-type diuretic
         drug

Proceed to full dose if necessary or desirable

Note: Additional substitutions may be made at this point.*

IF TARGET BLOOD PRESSURE GOAL IS NOT ACHIEVED:

STEP 3   Add a vasodilator (Hydralazine,
         or in resistant cases, minoxidil)

IF TARGET BLOOD PRESSURE GOAL IS NOT ACHIEVED:

STEP 4   Add guanethidine monosulfate

* An angiotensin-converting enzyme inhibitor may be substituted at Steps 2, 3, or 4 if side effects limit use of other agents or if they are ineffective. Calcium-channel blockers have not been officially approved for hypertension, but they may be acceptable as Step 2 or 3 drugs.

11
The Role of the Patient

We have said this many times before, but it bears repeating: The treatment of hypertension is a lifelong proposition. And the key to successful treatment is an educated patient who forms an effective working partnership with his or her physician and other members of the treatment team.

No two hypertensive patients are alike; therefore it follows that no two treatment programs are exactly the same. The majority of patients with mild to moderate hypertension can keep their blood pressure under control by taking one or two pills a day and following the life-style modifications—weight control, sodium restriction, stopping smoking, stress management, and so forth—outlined in earlier chapters. Some patients can get by without any pills, while others may need a combination of drugs that involves a more complicated regimen.

Intensive patient education is a central focus of hypertension treatment at the Cleveland Clinic. As explained by Dr. Vidt: "Most newly diagnosed hypertensive patients are shocked to learn that they have a serious disease. Ordinarily, they do not feel sick. Many learn about their high blood pressure after the development of some other problem, such as angina or a heart attack. Others may see their doctor about a weight problem or some other unrelated disorder, only to find out that they have high blood pressure. One of the first tasks is to reassure the patient. Hypertension is a serious disease but it is one that can be controlled a lot easier than many other chronic diseases, such as arthritis."

Effective treatment of high blood pressure requires considerable teamwork. The most important member of the team is the patient, since this is the person who is responsible for following the day-to-day regimen. The physician is another key member of the team. Without a smooth patient/physician working partnership, the chances of failure are high. Other members of the team may include other physicians to supervise treatment of concomitant problems, such as diabetes. A registered dietitian may be called upon for dietary counseling. Patients also may be referred to a stop-smoking program for help in giving up cigarettes. A psychologist may be consulted for help in coping with stress. Problems of alcohol abuse should be recognized and confronted, and patients often require help in quitting from Alcoholics Anonymous or a similar group.

The pharmacist is another important team member, and one who is often overlooked by both physician and patient. A pharmacist who keeps a record of patient medications, including over-the-counter drugs, can help ward off serious drug interactions. He or she also can answer questions about a specific drug, and spot common areas of noncompliance. Suppose, for example, that a patient is to take a drug twice a day. The prescription calls for sixty pills, but two months go by before it is renewed. Obviously, the patient is taking only half the recommended dosage, and this may explain why a certain drug regimen is not adequately controlling the blood pressure.

Cleveland Clinic physicians have found that enlisting other health professionals—nurse clinicians, physician assistants, health educators, dietitians, among others—to work directly with hypertensive patients is invaluable. "Very often, these other health professionals establish a very good rapport with patients," Dr. Gifford says. "They also have more time to talk to patients than physicians, and patients will often ask them questions or tell them of problems that they hesitate to discuss with their doctors."

Patient education at the Cleveland Clinic is approached with the same sort of precision and scientific study as prevails in treatment programs. Typically, once a diagnosis of hypertension is established, a Cleveland Clinic patient will be sent to the Department of Patient Education. This is one of the Clinic's newer departments, founded in 1975 under the direction of Dr. Penn Skillern. In addition to meeting with trained health educators, patients view an audiovisual program designed specifically to provide a working understanding of what is involved in high blood pressure. There is a brief quiz, which gives both the patient and the patient educator an idea of where more information is needed. Questions range from a very simple "Another name for high blood pressure is _____" to more sophisticated ones, such as: "One theory linking high blood pressure with hardening of the arteries is that high blood pressure causes rough spots in artery walls and these roughened areas collect _____ [cholesterol] or other deposits. The vessels become less elastic and the passage through which blood flows becomes _____ [narrowed]."

The six-step audiovisual program may take forty-five minutes or longer to complete. There is then time to talk to the health educator, to go over areas that still are not clear. The patient then may be asked to take a post-test to pinpoint misconceptions or misunderstandings.

ROLE OF THE FAMILY

Other family members are often key members of the team effort. "It's important that a spouse understand the nature of the disease," says Dr. Vidt. Some become overly anxious; others do not understand that high blood pressure is potentially serious and requires diligent lifelong treatment.

"Very often, we can enlist a family member to help a patient comply with treatment," explains Connie Sersig, a Clinic patient educator. "Some people simply cannot remember to take their medication, but if they are gently reminded by a family member, the problem disappears. Others need the feeling that they are not alone; they are more apt to stick to a diet or to exercise regularly if others are involved."

Mrs. Olds, one of the patients described in chapter 2, is a good example. She had never given much thought to exercise until, at her husband's urging, they both joined a health club. "He likes to go for long walks," Mrs. Olds explains, "but I have circulatory problems in my legs and simply cannot walk for more than a couple of blocks." The solution? Daily swimming, which both the Olds enjoy.

Mr. Rhodes has found his family very helpful in helping him follow his diet. "I used to be one of those people who added a generous sprinkle of salt before even tasting," he recalls. "One of the first things my wife did was remove the salt shaker from the table. She also cut back on salt in cooking. I help with the shopping, but she's the one who taught me how to read labels to look for hidden salt. I don't think I would have made this kind of an effort on my own."

Weight control is still another area in which a group effort can make a big difference. Mrs. Olds recalls that she has had a lifelong weight problem. Finally, after undergoing coronary bypass surgery, she decided it was time to shed thirty pounds for good. "Both my husband and I saw a Clinic dietitian," she recalls. "For the first time, I really sat down and analyzed my diet. I had not realized that I tend to eat when under pressure. Again, my husband helped by suggesting other less destructive ways of coping with stress besides heading for the refrigerator."

Some families make the mistake of isolating the patient by putting him or her on a special diet, Ms. Sersig notes. "We try to encourage the entire family to eat the same healthful diet. Unless a person is on a very low-calorie diet or is on some other very restricted regimen, there is no reason why the entire family cannot enjoy the same foods. If a patient thinks that he or she is being deprived of what other family members are eating, it won't be long before the diet is forgotten."

THE POTENTIAL OF PREVENTION

Enlisting other family members in the treatment of high blood pressure has an important added advantage; namely, the possibility of preventing it from developing in your children. Numerous studies have found that children of hypertensive parents are highly likely to develop the disease themselves. But there are also indications that early intervention may prevent this from happening. For example, sodium restriction in a child with a genetic tendency for hypertension may have an important preventive effect. The same goes for weight control and not smoking. Children of hypertensive parents should have their blood pressures measured regularly—at least once a year and oftener if they fall into the high-normal range. Early intervention for even a modest rise in blood pressure may prevent a later hypertension problem.

RECORD KEEPING

Cleveland Clinic patients are encouraged to monitor their own blood pressure at home and to keep a record of periodic readings. How often a patient takes his or her blood pressure depends upon individual circumstances. Patients starting a new drug regimen may be asked to measure their blood pressures daily or even two or three times a day. "This gives us a better idea of how the drugs are working and what dosage changes might be made," Dr. Gifford explains, adding: "It also saves a patient the time and expense of visiting a doctor or clinic just to have blood pressure measured."

Of course, periodic physician visits are still needed, especially when a treatment program is being established. But very often, reviewing a patient's record will enable a doctor to make appropriate changes based on a daily blood pressure record instead of the readings obtained during periodic office visits.

It is also reassuring to a patient to know that his or her blood pressure is under control. "There are instances, however, in which a patient can become too preoccupied with measuring blood pressure and become overly alarmed by a rise of one or two points that may simply reflect a normal variation," Dr. Gifford cautions. "It is important for patients who do home monitoring to realize that it is the average blood pressures over a period of time that's important."

Home blood pressure monitoring is also helpful in identifying hyper-responders with labile hypertension—blood pressure that may be high when measured in a doctor's office, but normal at home or in other settings. Most patients can quickly learn how to take their own blood pressures, using either a regular sphygmomanometer and stethoscope or an electronic sphygmomanometer with a digital display of the blood pressure. (See "Monitoring Your Own Blood Pressure," p. 148.) Alternatively, a family member may be enlisted to measure the blood pressure.

A record of blood pressure readings should be kept by the patient or family member. The readings can be recorded on a chart similar to the one provided in Table 11.1. Recording weight at the same time is also helpful, both in helping a patient keep tabs on weight control, and also in spotting possible problems of fluid retention (edema). A rapid gain of five or six pounds may be due to a buildup of fluid rather than added body fat.

In addition to keeping blood pressure and weight records, it is also a good idea for patients to maintain their own treatment record. Of course, the treating physician keeps such a record, and this is usually available to a patient. But many people see more than one doctor. By assuming responsibility for maintaining a personal medical record, a patient can readily provide a physician with information about other illnesses, medications, previous treatment regimens, complications, and so forth. A sample personal medical record form is provided in Table 11.2.

Noting any symptoms that may be related to an adverse reaction from a drug also is an important part of personal record keeping. Very often, a patient does not associate a certain symptom with a drug. For example, a number of antihypertensive medications cause sexual problems, such as a loss in sexual desire or impotence. Patients often do not link these problems to their medication and are embarrassed to mention them to a doctor. In many instances, the problem is easily solved by adjusting the dosage or switching medication. Sometimes problems are caused by unwittingly mixing drugs or by drugs and foods that interact with each other. Again, a doctor or pharmacist reviewing a medication/adverse reaction record can quickly spot these interactions, which can be potentially dangerous or even life-threatening.

DISPELLING COMMON MYTHS

Despite the increased emphasis on patient and public education regarding high blood pressure, many common myths persist. These include:

MYTH: Older people need higher blood pressure to ensure that enough blood gets to the brain and to prevent senility.

FACT: Blood pressure tends to rise with age in this country, but this is not the normal course of events in population groups that do not share our high degree of arteriosclerosis (hardening of the arteries) and higher-than-average blood pressures at younger ages. A seventy-year-old person with a normal blood pressure reading of 120–130/80 to 85 is likely to live longer than a person whose blood pressure is 170/90 or 95. There is no evidence that the higher blood pressure is needed to supply the aging brain with added oxygen, nor is there any evidence that this helps prevent mental decline. In fact, ministrokes or transient ischemic attacks, which may be caused by high blood pressure, are a common cause of mental deterioration among older people.

MYTH: Eating garlic will lower high blood pressure.

FACT: There is some evidence that consuming large amounts of garlic juice may result in a modest lowering of blood pressure. But a person would have to consume a pound or more of garlic a day—something that makes garlic a highly unlikely treatment of high blood pressure.

MYTH: If you take antihypertensive drugs, you can consume all the salt you want.

FACT: Although modern antihypertensive drugs mean that the old rice/fruit diets, which are very low in sodium, are no longer necessary, they do not mean that patients can consume large amounts of salt with impunity. Reducing sodium consumption often means that the drugs will be more effective in lowering blood pressure, and that smaller dosages may be prescribed, thereby reducing the potential for adverse side effects.

MYTH: Once your blood pressure is under control, you can stop taking antihypertensive drugs.

FACT: Sometimes a patient can be weaned off drugs without having blood pressure go up, but this is the exception rather than the rule. Patients in this category are often people who had mild high blood pressure and who have lost weight, reduced sodium intake, increased exercise, and made other lifestyle changes that have helped control the blood pressure. Sometimes blood pressure will return to normal after a heart attack or coronary bypass surgery. But in all instances, patients should be carefully monitored because in a large percentage the blood pressure will eventually go back up.

MYTH: The prevalence of high blood pressure among Americans is due to our hectic stress-filled pace of life.

FACT: Stress raises blood pressure, but this is usually a temporary phenomenon; the blood pressure will return to normal when the stress is removed. It is unlikely that stress alone produces high blood pressure. Everyone lives with varying degrees of stress and tension; some people are subjected to extraordinary stresses without developing high blood pressure while others who have very few stresses will become hypertensive.

MYTH: Tranquilizers will lower blood pressure.

FACT: An occasional tranquilizer or sedative may be prescribed to overcome extreme anxiety or to help in coping with an unusual period of stress, such as the loss of a loved one. But tranquilizers do not lower blood pressure and are not recommended as part of an antihypertensive regimen.

MYTH: An occasional drink can help control blood pressure by making you feel more relaxed.

FACT: Alcohol may have a temporary relaxing effect for some people, but it does not help in the treatment of high blood pressure. In fact, heavy use of alcohol, defined as more than four or five drinks a day, can raise blood pressure. In addition, heavy alcohol use can damage the heart, liver, brain, and other vital organs. The extra calories in alcohol can add to a weight problem and increase the risk of certain nutritional deficiencies.

These are but a few of the common myths and misconceptions about high blood pressure. Whenever in doubt about any aspect about hypertension and its treatment, ask your doctor. Above all, never change a prescribed regimen on your own. Sometimes patients will suspect that a drug is causing a certain side effect and will discontinue taking it on their own. This can be a fatal mistake with some drugs, such as the beta blockers which must be withdrawn gradually. Others will become worried by a symptom or perhaps a rise in blood pressure measured at home and will increase their medication. Again, this can be a fatal mistake. Although the patient is the most important member of his or her treatment team, decisions about drug dosages and other therapies must be made by an experienced physician. It was a wise person who observed that a person who treats himself has a fool for a physician! Even a doctor who has high blood pressure will go to another physician to be treated.

In summary, the most important points to remember about the patient's role in controlling high blood pressure are:

- There is no cure for primary hypertension, therefore, treatment is almost always a lifelong undertaking.
- By working with your doctor and other health professionals, hypertension almost always can be controlled with a minimum of side effects.
- Bringing high blood pressure under control reduces the risk of premature death and minimizes the risk for heart attacks, strokes, kidney failure, and blindness.

TABLE 11.1. HYPERTENSION PATIENT RECORDING

HISTORY NUMBER |___|—|___|___|___|—|___|___|___|—|___|

PATIENT _____

		WEEK 1							WEEK 3			
	DATE	A.M.		P.M.		REMARKS		DATE	A.M.		P.M.	REMARKS
		L	S	L	S				L	S	L	S	
01							15						
02							16						
03							17						
04							18						
05							19						
06							20						
07							21						

		WEEK 2							WEEK 4			
	DATE	A.M.		P.M.		REMARKS		DATE	A.M.		P.M.	REMARKS
		L	S	L	S				L	S	L	S	
08							22						
09							23						
10							24						
11							25						
12							26						
13							27						
14							28						

TABLE 11.2. RECORD OF PHYSICIAN VISITS

Name _____

DATE	NAME OF DOCTOR	REASON FOR VISIT	RECOMMENDED THERAPY (DRUGS, ETC.)

TABLE 11.3. MEDICATION HISTORY

Name _____

DATE	NAME OF DRUG	PRESCRIBED BY	PRESCRIBED FOR	REACTION OR SIDE EFFECT

148

Managing Hypertension

MONITORING YOUR OWN BLOOD PRESSURE

Individual monitoring of blood pressure helps both physician and patient. It provides the doctor with a more complete record of readings under a variety of conditions (many patients find that their blood pressure readings are slightly lower when taken at home in a more relaxed atmosphere). Monitoring at home also helps assure the patient that his or her blood pressure is under control and lets the patient know when a trip to the doctor may be necessary.

Automatic blood pressure reading machines can be found in many local pharmacies and in other public places. Although these machines are not as accurate as the reading taken in the doctor's office or even those taken at home by the patient, they have convenience and low cost (eliminating the need to purchase equipment) in their favor, and the data supplied can be useful. These machines are easy to use; directions are usually printed on them.

But many patients choose to take their blood pressure with a sphygmomanometer and stethoscope at home. Following is a description of how to take your own blood pressure. Your doctor may also have some suggestions of his or her own.

- It is best to take your blood pressure in a quiet place, and, if possible, use your right arm for the measurement. Readings will be different while sitting, standing, or lying down. Dr. Gifford recommends that readings be taken while standing and sitting, but be sure to note your position for each reading in your record. The forearm should be positioned so that your upper arm (where the cuff will be placed) is about even with your heart. Find the brachial artery in the crook of your elbow by feeling for the pulse with your fingertips. This is where you will place the stethoscope after you have slipped the deflated cuff onto your arm. Use the ring and Velcro wrap to fit the cuff snugly over the upper arm. Place the stethoscope over the artery.
- Place the manometer (pressure gauge) where you can see it easily. Inflate the cuff slightly and listen through the stethoscope for the sound of your pulse. You may have to experiment a little until you find the positioning that allows you to hear the pulse best. Then inflate the cuff about 30 points (millimeters of mercury) above your expected systolic pressure. (Use your last reading or the reading taken in the

Continued

doctor's office. For example, if your last blood pressure reading was 120/80, inflate the cuff to 150 or 155.)

- Once the pressure in the cuff is greater than your systolic pressure, the cuff will act as a tourniquet, cutting off the blood supply. Keeping your eye on the gauge, gradually release the pressure in the cuff. It will take some practice to learn to pace this correctly, so that the pressure falls 2 or 3 points for each heartbeat.

- As long as the pressure in the cuff is higher than your systolic blood pressure, you will not hear your pulse. The first pulse beat you do hear, then, indicates that the cuff pressure is just below your systolic blood pressure. Note the reading on the pressure gauge at the first sound of your pulse. This is your systolic pressure reading.

- To get your diastolic reading, continue to let air out of the cuff. The sound of your pulse will get louder as more blood is allowed through the artery. Then, as the cuff pressure approaches your diastolic reading and the tourniquet effect lessens, the sound of your pulse will start to fade. Listen carefully: The gauge level at the last pulse you hear is your diastolic reading.

- Record both the systolic and diastolic readings as well as the date and time of the measurement. Other pertinent data to include in your record may be your weight and pulse, any medications taken, any unusual physical activity, emotional stress or, for women, menstrual period. Bring your complete record with you each time you see your physician.

12
Treating Resistant Hypertension

Most cases of hypertension can be controlled by the regimens outlined in the preceding chapters. Occasionally, however, there are patients who follow their doctor's instructions to the letter and still have problems. Such cases are referred to as resistant hypertension. There also are patients whose hypertension treatment is complicated by other diseases or circumstances, making it more difficult to treat.

Since the Cleveland Clinic is one of the world's major referral centers and is known for expertise in treating hypertension, its doctors see a greater-than-average number of patients with resistant hypertension. Sometimes all that is required is a little judicious detective work to determine whether the cause is a failure to use the drugs properly or other factors, such as excessive salt consumption. In other instances, further testing may be needed to determine whether the hypertension is secondary to some other disease. Most often, the problems can be solved by changing the drug regimen. The following case histories of Cleveland Clinic patients illustrate the kinds of problems that may be encountered and their solutions.

Mary M., a twenty-nine-year-old schoolteacher, was referred to the Cleveland Clinic because of severe hypertension that had developed over the previous six months and which was not being controlled by multiple drugs. Her blood pressure was 194/140. For three months she had been troubled by severe headaches that were not relieved by aspirin or other nonprescription painkillers. She also had episodes of nausea and vomiting.

She finally consulted her family doctor, who discovered her blood pressure was 240/110. She had evidence of blood vessel hemorrhages in her eyes. Her blood pressure had been normal eight months earlier when she had her last checkup following the birth of her second child. Both her pregnancies had been normal and she had never had high blood pressure before. Her mother, however, had been under treatment for hypertension for about fifteen years.

Because Mary's blood pressure was so high and she had evidence of eye damage despite the relatively recent onset of the hypertension, her doctor admitted her to a community hospital for treatment and kidney tests. Immediate treatment with intravenous diazoxide, a vasodilator drug that is used in hypertensive emergencies, lowered her blood pressure. The kidney tests showed no abnormalities, ruling out her doctor's suspicion of hypertension caused by renal problems. Her other tests also were normal. But when the intravenous drug was stopped, her blood pressure went back up.

She was referred to the Cleveland Clinic for further kidney tests and treatment of her hypertension. During her initial interview, Clinic physicians learned that she relied on an oral contraceptive for birth control. After reviewing her history and analyzing her laboratory tests, they decided to wait before doing further kidney studies. Instead, they prescribed a Step 3 drug regimen (a thiazide diuretic, a beta blocker, and a vasodilator) to lower her blood pressure. They also instructed her to stop taking the pill immediately and to avoid other drugs, such as the nonsteroidal anti-inflammatory drugs she sometimes took for menstrual cramps, that might raise blood pressure. Her family doctor also had overlooked this as a possible cause of her hypertension since she had used the pill for a total of four years. After three months, her headaches and hypertension had disappeared. She was able to gradually stop the antihypertensive drugs. She did not resume use of an oral contraceptive since it seemed clear that this had been the cause of her hypertension.

In commenting on this case history, Dr. Gifford notes that it is full of exceptions to the rules. "This patient's family doctor knew that oral contraceptives sometimes cause hypertension in women; he had discounted them in this case because she had been on the pill for several years. Usually, if the pill is going to cause high blood pressure, it does so within a few months. But there have been other cases like this one in which hypertension suddenly develops after years of pill use." Dr. Gifford also noted that the blood pressure rises produced by oral contraceptives are usually modest, only 5 or 10 mm Hg. But in rare instances these and other drugs can produce very severe, progressive hypertension. "This young woman was fortunate in one sense," Dr. Gifford adds. "Sometimes drug-induced blood pressure does not return to normal after the drugs are discontinued. Mary was able to be weaned off her antihypertensive drugs in a relatively short time with no further problems."

Mrs. Graham, a fifty-five-year-old department store executive, also was referred to the Cleveland Clinic for evaluation of resistant hypertension. Like Mary, she developed severely high blood pressure in a short time. Persistent headaches prompted her to see her doctor, who was surprised to find that her blood pressure was 220/120. When he had last seen her, about fifteen months earlier, it had been 110/70. She was sent to a local hospital for treatment and tests, including X-ray studies of her kidneys. These were normal. She was started on three antihypertensive drugs: a thiazide diuretic, a beta blocker, and a vasodilator. Despite following the regimen faithfully, her diastolic blood pressure remained at 110 or higher.

When she came to the Cleveland Clinic, she told doctors that she had suffered chronic fatigue for the last three months. She also said she was very worried. Her mother had died of hypertension and kidney failure at the age of seventy-two, and her sister had died of a stroke a year earlier.

At the time of her visit, her blood pressure was 180/110. Her eyes showed blood vessel constriction, but no damage. Her heart and lungs seemed normal. Her blood and urine studies were normal except for a low potassium level, which was surprising since her thiazide dosage was low enough to avoid potassium depletion. Further studies of Mrs. Graham's kidneys revealed that the left one was normal but that the right one was shrunken and the renal artery leading to it did not show up on the X rays. Based on this and renin studies, the doctors concluded that the problem was caused by a blockage of her right renal artery, a disorder known as renovascular hypertension. To compensate for the diminished blood flow, the kidney produced more renin, which in turn set in motion the production of other blood chemicals that raise blood pressure. Since the renal artery was blocked, even with the high blood pressure, it was being starved. So it produced even more renin and higher blood pressure.

The kidney proved too damaged to save; it was removed and the remaining healthy kidney continued to function for both. In a short time, Mrs. Graham's blood pressure was again normal and her other symptoms disappeared.

"Mrs. Graham's family physician had suspected renovascular hypertension but had discounted it when the first kidney studies looked normal," Dr. Gifford explained. "But in the five or six months that passed between those first X rays and our tests, the right artery had become totally blocked and the kidney had shrunk to about half its original size. False-negative results are unusual in X-ray studies, but they do happen. The lesson here is if the symptoms continue to arouse suspicion, further investigation is needed."

Robert L., a forty-seven-year-old Ohio businessman, had been treated for hypertension for at least ten years. His mother had had hypertension and his father had died of a heart attack at age fifty-two. Robert had had no major illnesses except for two bouts of depression, which had been overcome with an antidepressant drug.

Initially, Robert had been put on a diuretic. When this failed to control his blood pressure, another drug, reserpine, had been added. This brought his blood pressure down from 170/110 to 140/85. But within six months, the blood pressure was back up to 150–170/95–110. He had missed a followup appointment but finally went to his doctor accompanied by his wife, who was worried about his other symptoms: difficulty sleeping, loss of appetite, disinterest in almost everything that had formerly given him pleasure—sex, his children, business, even Ohio State's (his alma mater) winning football team. His doctor quickly determined that he was suffering another bout of depression and that he had quietly stopped taking his antihypertensive medications. An antidepressant drug was prescribed and the hypertension regimen was changed; the reserpine was dropped and the thiazide dosage was increased. When they failed to lower the blood pressure sufficiently, another drug, guanethidine, was added. But his blood pressure remained unchanged.

After reviewing Robert's medication history, Cleveland Clinic physicians quickly concluded that most of his problems stemmed from inappropriate choices of drugs. "He was taking a high dose of reserpine, which probably should not have been prescribed at all, given the patient's previous bouts with depression. Depression is a possible side effect of reserpine, and it may have precipitated the recurrence. Substituting guanethidine for the reserpine was also a poor choice because the antidepressant that Robert was taking interacts with guanethidine, diminishing its antihypertensive effect."

In Robert's new regimen, the diuretic and antidepressant drugs were continued and the guanethidine was stopped. Since beta blockers and some of the other traditional Step 2 drugs, such as methyldopa and clonidine, might interact with antidepressants and may themselves produce depression, the doctors sought an alternative drug without these effects. "In this case, we could try one of the beta blockers that does not enter the central nervous system or use a drug like prazosin," Dr. Gifford explains. Prazosin was the choice and in a short time the desired blood pressure goal was reached and Robert also recovered from his depression.

"He has continued to do well over the last two years," Dr. Gifford reports, adding that this particular case history illustrates several important points. "Large numbers of hypertensive patients go for years with inadequate treatment. Robert had been treated with a thiazide alone for years without his blood pressure becoming normal. Then when another drug was added, it turned out to be one that produced a predictable side effect, given his past episodes of depression. When we first saw him, the patient simply was not taking his medication. Whenever a drug regimen is not working, one of the first tasks is to determine whether the patient really is taking the medications as directed."

Dr. Gifford stresses that increased awareness of the serious consequences of hypertension along with better drugs with fewer side effects has greatly improved the problem of patients' failing to follow a prescribed regimen. "But the problem of patient compliance has not disappeared," he adds. "It's unfair to blame noncompliance on the patient alone; the doctor also has a responsibility to follow up and to make sure the regimen is one that the patient can comfortably live with."

WHEN HYPERTENSION OCCURS WITH OTHER DISEASES

The treatment of hypertension is often complicated by other diseases, sometimes related to the high blood pressure and at other times the two may be independent of each other. Very often, different regimens must be tried to arrive at one that will not counteract the treatment for the other disorder and, at the same time, control the hypertension.

Patients who have both diabetes and high blood pressure are a common example, since the two diseases often go together. These patients are particularly vulnerable to heart and kidney problems, since both disorders damage these organs. The problem is further complicated by the fact that some of the drugs used to treat hypertension may make the diabetes more difficult to control. Beta blockers and diuretics both may raise blood glucose. Beta blockers also may interfere with the body's ability to respond to an insulin overdose by masking the characteristic warning signs of an insulin reaction and also by prolonging the low blood sugar (hypoglycemia). Most patients with diabetes can compensate for these effects and learn how to control both their diseases, but potential problems should be discussed with the doctor in advance so the patient will know how to handle them.

Hypertension and coronary artery disease are two other disorders that often coexist. Some of the same drugs, such as beta blockers, are used to treat both. But there are instances in which this may be contraindicated. If the patient also has congestive heart failure or heart block, a disruption of the heart's electrical impulses, a beta blocker may not be a good choice of drug. Vasodilators may precipitate attacks of angina in patients with coronary disease. Calcium-channel blockers should be used cautiously, if at all, by patients with congestive heart failure.

As we have seen, special care must be taken in selecting antihypertensive drugs when treating patients susceptible to depression because some drugs may trigger depression. But this is not the only disorder that may be triggered or worsened by antihypertensive drugs. Some beta blockers may worsen asthma or other respiratory disorders. Thiazides are often ineffective when given to patients who have failing kidneys; these diuretics also may trigger attacks of gout. In rare cases, methyldopa may cause liver damage and should not be taken by people with liver disorders. (For more on the side effects of antihypertensive agents, see Table 10.2, "Adverse Drug Effects," in chapter 10.)

There are a number of drugs that may increase blood pressure. MAO inhibitors, which are sometimes prescribed to treat depression, may precipitate a hypertensive crisis if consumed with foods that contain tyramine, such as aged cheese, beer, or Chianti. Nonsteroidal anti-inflammatory drugs, which are frequently used to treat arthritis, can raise high blood pressure, probably because these agents block the production of prostaglandins, hormone-like substances that regulate blood pressure. Cortisone and other steroids and, as described in the case of Mary S., oral contraceptives also may increase blood pressure, probably because they promote salt and water retention. The hypertensive effects of these drugs are usually minor, but some patients may react more than others. Also, the drugs may reduce the effectiveness of certain antihypertensive medications.

People with high blood pressure should always read the labels or package inserts of all medications, both prescription and over-the-counter. Asthma medications, nonprescription cold pills, appetite suppressants, and other drugs that work through the sympathetic nervous system can raise blood pressure. Their hypertensive effect is increased when they are taken with beta blockers, MAO inhibitors, or drugs like nonsteroidal anti-inflammatory medications, which inhibit prostaglandin production.

Alcohol is still another commonly used substance that has been shown to increase blood pressure. The more alcohol consumed, the more pronounced the hypertensive effects. A number of illicit or abused drugs, including cocaine, amphetamines, and PCP, may affect blood pressure.

Most people are aware that salty foods may aggravate hypertension, but not many know that large amounts of licorice can also produce high blood pressure. Licorice contains glyceric acid, a salt-retaining compound. People with high blood pressure should avoid licorice, or eat the kind made with artificial flavor. Large amounts of vitamins E and D can also raise blood pressure.

From this long list of cautions, you might be tempted to conclude that there are "booby traps" lurking on every plate or in every pill bottle. This is hardly the case. As stressed throughout the book, the vast majority of patients with high blood pressure can keep the disease under control and live productive, normal lives. But caution is advised. When blood pressure rises even though a patient has carefully followed his or her prescribed regimen, the reason can occasionally be traced to the use of a medication or a food.

13
Hypertension in Children

Hypertension most often develops when people are in their thirties and forties, but the disease sometimes occurs at much younger ages. Studies in recent years have found that 1 to 2 percent of children have high blood pressure. Most childhood hypertension occurs during adolescence, but high blood pressure has been found even in infants. Very high blood pressure in a young child is usually due to an underlying cause, such as a kidney disorder or a congenital defect of the aorta. But doctors are becoming increasingly aware that youngsters also may have mild primary hypertension, which places them in a special high-risk category for premature heart disease and other consequences of high blood pressure.

Until recently, blood pressure usually was not routinely measured in young children. Now, however, pediatricians are urged to make blood pressure measurement a part of routine pediatric checkups, beginning at an early age. Dr. Edward Kass, a researcher at Harvard Medical School, was one of the first physicians to study the prevalence of childhood hypertension. He and his colleagues set out to confirm whether hypertension was hereditary, as seemed apparent from reviewing the family histories of people with high blood pressure, and, if so, when in life the disease developed. Their study involved measuring the blood pressures of newborn infants, and also checking the urine for the presence of kallikrein, an enzyme that occurs in low levels in hypertensive adults. Urine studies of children in Dr. Kass's study showed that those with higher-than-normal blood pressures also had low levels of kallikrein.

Some of the Harvard findings were expected. Babies born to parents who had high blood pressure tended to be at the high end of the normal scale. In following these children over the next decade, Dr. Kass has confirmed that they stay in the high group. (Table 13.1 outlines the upper limits of normal blood pressure in children of different ages.) Similar findings have emerged from other studies. One of the most extensive such studies has been conducted in Bogalusa, Louisiana. In this long-term study, Dr. Gerald Berenson of the Louisiana State Medical School and his colleagues have measured the blood pressures of virtually every child in Bogalusa at least nine times. They have found that black children have significantly higher blood pressures at an earlier age than white children. Hypertension is more common among blacks than whites, and this study indicates that it begins at an early age. Dr. Berenson also has found that obese children and those who are tall for their age tend to have higher blood pressures than those who are thin and smaller.

TABLE 13.1: UPPER LIMITS OF NORMAL BLOOD PRESSURE IN CHILDREN

AGE (YEARS)	BLOOD PRESSURE
6 or younger	110/75
6 to 10	120/80
10 to 14	125/85
14 to 18	135/90

Thus, it is possible to identify a large percentage of people who are likely to eventually develop hypertension early in life. The importance of this is two-fold: Children at the high end of the blood pressure scale probably should be followed more closely than those with more average readings because they are more likely to develop the disease at an early age; also, it may be well to concentrate preventive efforts on these children to see if their tendency to hypertension can somehow be aborted. Animal studies have found, for example, that offspring of a strain of rats with a high susceptibility to hypertension do not develop the disease when fed a low-salt diet. In contrast, littermates fed a high-salt diet do go on to become hypertensive.

A major problem is a lack of knowledge about the development of primary hypertension during childhood. There is also the problem of falsely labeling a child as having a serious disease—there are still some doctors who contend that mild hypertension is not a disease per se because it does not produce symptoms and most people can live normal lives for fifteen or twenty years or more without encountering problems. Is there really a benefit in worrying a child and his or her parents about a condition that may never progress beyond high normal? There is also the question of when to initiate treatment for mild primary hypertension in a child. As yet, there are no clear answers to these important questions, but guidelines for dealing with childhood hypertension are being formulated at leading institutions, such as the Cleveland Clinic.

"Most of the hypertensive children we see have seriously high blood pressures," Dr. Vidt says. "Our initial response is to look for possible causes of the high blood pressure." The first examination is much the same as for an adult hypertensive. Particular attention is paid to the family medical history. If parents or other close relatives have a background of primary hypertension, it may indicate early onset of this type of high blood pressure in a child. Special care should be taken in measuring a child's blood pressure, including making sure that the cuff is the proper size. Using a cuff that is too narrow or too small may produce falsely elevated readings, while too large a cuff may give readings that are too low.

Like adults, some children may be hyperreactors, with a high blood pressure reading in the doctor's office and normal blood pressures at other times. Therefore, as with adults, several readings and physician visits are needed before arriving at a diagnosis of hypertension unless the blood pressure is severely elevated and there are other symptoms.

During the physical examination, physicians look for any signs of organ damage to the heart, kidney, and eyes. They also look for any clues that may indicate a cause of the high blood pressure. For example, the child's genitalia are examined for any signs of premature sexual development or masculinization, which may indicate a congenital disorder of the adrenal glands. The kidneys are examined for any signs of tumors or other abnormalities. Neurological responses are carefully tested. Conditions such as convulsions, may turn out to be related to unsuspected hypertension.

The heart and pulses also are carefully examined. An EKG is usually advisable. Blood pressure should be measured in both arms and also in the legs. A child who has high systolic pressure and strong pulses in the arms and upper part of the body but lower blood pressure and weak or absent pulses in the lower part of the body may have a congenital abnormality called coarctation of the aorta. In this abnormality, there is an infolding at some point in the aorta, causing a narrowing of this major artery. There also may be an aneurysm, a weakened segment of the blood vessel that balloons out and is at risk of rupturing. Coarctation of the aorta may cause an enlarged heart or congestive heart failure.

A number of laboratory tests of blood and urine are recommended to see if there are signs of kidney disease. Endocrine or hormonal abnormalities also can cause hypertension. One example is hyperaldosteronism, a rare condition in which the adrenal glands produce excessive aldosterone, a hormone that raises blood pressure. The extent of the testing usually depends upon the severity of the hypertension and the age of the child. A very young child with severely elevated blood pressure is more likely to have secondary hypertension and more extensive testing is justified in these youngsters than in an older child with mild high blood pressure and signs pointing to primary hypertension.

Children with diabetes are highly likely to also have high blood pressure.

Some studies have found that up to 80 percent of diabetic patients also have high blood pressure. Since insulin-dependent or juvenile diabetes often begins in childhood, the high blood pressure may indicate the onset of diabetes. However, there are other more important symptoms, such as excessive thirst, fatigue, and weight loss.

Childhood primary hypertension appears to become more common as children get older. Surveys of high school students in several cities, including New York, St. Louis, Washington, D.C., and Tecumseh, Michigan, have found that 8 to 20 percent of the students studied have higher than normal blood pressure. Most of the readings fall into the mild or high normal ranges but are of concern because of future implications.

Adolescents sometimes develop a transient type of mild high blood pressure. The reason for this is unknown, although some experts think it may be related to hormonal changes and the adolescent growth spurt. After a year or two, the blood pressure may return to normal levels. But these people should be checked at least yearly in adulthood since a number of studies have shown that they are likely to develop high blood pressure later in life. Dr. Ralph Paffenberger, a Harvard Medical School researcher, looked up the blood pressure measurements of young men entering college at Harvard and the University of Pennsylvania in past years and then tried to determine whether these single measurements had any bearing on their future health or longevity. He found that the students who had systolic blood pressures of 130 or higher had a 60 percent higher death rate from heart attacks over the subsequent four decades than their counterparts with lower blood pressure readings.

APPROACHES TO CHILDHOOD HYPERTENSION

As noted earlier, there are no specific guidelines for treating childhood hypertension. If the high blood pressure is secondary to kidney disease or some other identifiable disorder, treating the underlying cause can possibly cure the hypertension. In approaching mild primary hypertension in children, a growing number of experts advise following a course similar to that recommended for adults.

"If the hypertension is mild or if it is the systolic pressure that is elevated, we advise nondrug treatment first, similar to what we outline for adults," Dr. Gifford explains. This means cutting back on salt consumption, weight control, exercise, and not smoking. At the Cleveland Clinic, adult hypertensives are counseled about salt reduction and other dietary changes that may lower their risk of cardiovascular disease. "We encourage the entire family to adopt a low-salt, low-fat diet," says Dr. Vidt. The physicians and dietitians stress to patients that their children have a higher than average risk of developing high blood pressure and its consequences, and that a prudent prevention program started early in life may spare them their parent's disease. "We also have found that it is easier for a patient to stick to his or her diet if the entire family is eating the same food," Dr. Vidt adds.

Cleveland Clinic physicians also emphasize the importance of not smoking. "Although smoking does not increase the incidence of hypertension," Dr. Gifford notes, "it is a major risk factor for later heart disease, chronic lung problems, and cancer." The Framingham Heart Study and other studies have found that hypertensive patients who also smoke have a higher incidence of heart attacks than nonsmokers with the same blood pressure.

Once established, a cigarette habit is very hard to break. "It's far better to never start smoking than to try to stop," Dr. Gifford observes. Increasingly, schoolchildren are taking up smoking—a factor that is of growing concern to public health officials. Studies have found that most people who smoke start in the seventh grade, or at about the age of twelve or thirteen. A few years ago, Dr. Henry Blackburn and his colleagues at the University of Minnesota undertook a major study of smoking among schoolchildren with the aim of developing an effective smoking prevention program. "We found that at the beginning of the seventh grade, about 11 percent of the children use cigarettes at least occasionally, but by the end of that grade, the figure jumps to about a third, which is about the percentage of adult smokers," Dr. Blackburn explains. "The objective is to prevent their starting. The longer we can keep a youngster from taking up a cigarette habit, the more likely that person is to be a nonsmoker as an adult."

The Minnesota Smoking Prevention Program, widely hailed as a prototype for school health programs, relies on teenage attitudes and concerns. "We know that adolescents have little concern over what is going to happen ten or twenty years down the road," Dr. Blackburn explains. "They are much more concerned about immediate objectives and consequences. They also are very concerned about peer pressures. If a thirteen-year-old thinks 'everyone is doing it,' he or she wants to do it too." The Minnesota program, which has been tested in the Minneapolis school system for more than five years, identifies and enlists peer leaders—the youngsters who are most admired by their classmates—to conduct the smoking prevention program. The messages are not so much about future health consequences as more immediate concerns: bad breath, adverse effects on athletic ability, smelly hair, unattractive consequences for the skin—the sort of things youngsters of that age worry about. The leaders also emphasize that "not everyone is doing it"; two thirds of teenagers and adults alike do not smoke.

Does this approach work? In the Minneapolis school tests of the program, at the end of the seventh grade, about 11 to 13 percent of the youngsters who participated in the program smoked—about the same percentage as at the beginning of the year. In contrast, about 33 percent of youngsters in comparable classes that did not have the program smoked at the end of the seventh grade. It is not known how many of the youngsters will later take up smoking, but as Dr. Blackburn notes, "Every year we can keep children from starting smoking, the less likely they are to start."

With the mounting evidence that high blood pressure may begin early in life, the increased attention to measuring the blood pressure of young children is an important step in identifying youngsters who may be at special risk. Salt restriction, weight control, and a prudent life-style may well help prevent the development of adult hypertension among children whose blood pressures fall into the high range.

14
Special Cases of Secondary Hypertension

About 90 to 95 percent of all patients with high blood pressure have primary, or essential, hypertension, meaning that there is no evident cause of the disease. Most of this book has been devoted to this large majority. But that still leaves 5 to 10 percent of patients—a considerable number considering there are up to sixty million Americans with high blood pressure—who have secondary hypertension. In these patients, the high blood pressure is caused by some other underlying problem. Sometimes the high blood pressure can be traced to life-style factors, such as the use of birth control pills or alcohol. In such instances, removing the underlying cause usually will solve the problem. Following are some of the other more common causes of secondary hypertension.

PHEOCHROMOCYTOMA

Pheochromocytoma is a rare condition in which tumors that produce adrenal hormones (catecholamines) develop. The major catecholamines are epinephrine and norepinephrine, commonly referred to as stress hormones. Epinephrine is a powerful heart stimulant; norepinephrine raises blood pressure.

Hypertension is one of the most common symptoms of pheochromocytoma. The high blood pressure may be persistent or occasional. Other symptoms may include rapid heartbeat, chest pains, headaches, tremor, sweating, feelings of agitation or anxiety, pallor, cold, clammy skin, visual disturbances, nausea and vomiting, and fainting when standing up (postural hypotension). There also may be sugar in the urine and speeded-up metabolism.

The tumors often develop in the adrenal glands, which rest atop the kidneys, but they may occur in other parts of the body that contain cells derived from the neural crest, such as along the course of the aorta, in the brain, the genitourinary system, or in the carotid body. The tumors are usually so small that they cannot be detected by feeling, but, often, pressure applied over the area can provoke an attack of very high blood pressure, rapid heartbeat, and other symptoms.

A diagnosis of pheochromocytoma usually can be based on urinary tests for high levels of the metabolic by-products of epinephrine and norepinephrine and other biochemical abnormalities. Computerized tomographic (CT) scanning and other X-ray studies usually can locate the tumors.

The preferred treatment is surgical removal of the tumors. Drugs, such as beta- and alpha-adrenergic blocking agents, may be given to control the high blood pressure and to allow the patient to be in as good a condition as possible to withstand the surgery. Removal of the tumors usually cures the hypertension.

RENAL HYPERTENSION

All types of chronic kidney disease may cause high blood pressure. As discussed in earlier chapters, the kidney plays a key role in regulating blood pressure. Any disorder that reduces the blood supply to one or both kidneys can cause a rise in blood pressure.

Kidney studies are indicated in hypertensive patients who fail to respond to treatment, who have other signs of renal failure, or who are very young. A kidney disease also should be suspected in high blood pressure that comes on very suddenly and is not related to other causes, such as the use of drugs that may induce hypertension. Kidney infections, stones, obstruction, tumors, and constricture of the renal arteries or other blood vessels are among the causes of renal hypertension.

Malignant or progressive hypertension is also frequently caused by kidney disorders. Patients with malignant hypertension usually have very high diastolic blood pressures, frequently 130 to 170 mm Hg or even higher. They often have signs of an enlarged heart and buildup of fluid in the lungs. An examination of the eyes is particularly revealing. The retina usually shows the presence of spots that look like cotton wool, vascular changes, and swelling of the optic disk (papilledema).

Malignant hypertension requires prompt emergency treatment since it can quickly develop into a fatal stroke, kidney failure, or congestive heart failure. The use of powerful antihypertensive drugs and diagnosis and treatment of any underlying kidney cause of the hypertension usually will bring the blood pressure under control.

HYPERTENSION IN PREGNANCY

High blood pressure during pregnancy poses a special hazard to both the mother and the fetus. It also may be a sign of toxemia, a serious complication that sometimes develops toward the end of pregnancy and which can progress to severe hypertension, kidney failure, convulsions, and even death.

If a woman is hypertensive before becoming pregnant, or if high blood pressure develops early in pregnancy, special diligence is required to make sure that the blood pressure is controlled. Even mild high blood pressure can result in a small birth-weight baby, fetal death, or prematurity. Methyldopa is the antihypertensive drug most commonly prescribed during pregnancy. In the past, pregnant women with high blood pressure were usually treated in the hospital, often for many weeks or even months. This usually is not necessary now, but a pregnant hypertensive must see her physician frequently and should also monitor her own blood pressure at home.

COARCTATION OF THE AORTA

Coarctation of the aorta is a congenital defect in which part of the aorta is severely narrowed or even closed. It is characterized by high blood pressure and strong pulses in the upper part of the body, and low blood pressure and weak or absent pulses in the lower part of the body. In some instances, the disorder becomes apparent early in life; in others, it may not show up until the second or third decades, or even later.

Treatment involves surgery to repair the constricted aorta. Sometimes if the abnormality is discovered in infancy or early childhood, the narrowed portion of the aorta can be widened by balloon angioplasty, a technique in which a catheter with a balloon attached is threaded into the aorta and the balloon is then inflated at the point of narrowing.

HYPERTENSION RELATED TO EXCESS ALDOSTERONE

Aldosterone is a steroid hormone that controls electrolyte metabolism. Its secretion is regulated by the renin-angiotensin system; its function is to increase the excretion of potassium and conserve sodium and chloride. An excess of aldosterone may be caused by adrenal tumors or hyperplasia. The hypertension may be accompanied by other symptoms, such as muscle weakness.

As noted earlier, most of these disorders are quite rare. Typically, doctors do not look for these or other causes of secondary hypertension unless there are other clues. Sometimes a careful review of the patient's symptoms and other medical problems will point to secondary hypertension; more frequently, investigations for a cause of the high blood pressure are justified if the hypertension persists despite a full course of treatment that would normally lower the high blood pressure.

Afterword: A Look to the Future

During my years as a physician, I have witnessed tremendous advances in the detection, diagnosis, and treatment of hypertension. Patients who were once doomed to an early death from malignant high blood pressure are now being effectively treated and returned to normal, productive lives. Indeed, malignant hypertension has become a relatively rare disease.

A host of new drugs and improved understanding of hypertension are helping the millions of Americans with mild to moderate hypertension, preventing the more severe forms of the disease and also the complications that were so common in the past. As noted in this book, the incidence of fatal strokes has dropped by 45 percent in recent years, and our improved treatment of high blood pressure is also a major factor in the declining death toll from heart attacks.

As impressive as these gains are, I am confident that they are only a beginning. As I write this, continuing research at the Cleveland Clinic and elsewhere is developing even more effective drugs. We still do not know what causes primary hypertension, but every year we are gaining new insight into the disease that, in the future, may enable us to prevent high blood pressure in an increasing number of people. Finally, there is little doubt in my mind that our changing life-style is having an impact, not only on hypertension, but on other forms of cardiovascular disease as well. The increased emphasis on fitness, a prudent diet, stress management, and other life-style modifications already is beginning to pay off.

At the Cleveland Clinic, we have long recognized that the patient is perhaps the most important member of the treatment team. Our physicians and other health-care professionals can prescribe treatments and recommend dietary and other life-style changes directed to controlling high blood pressure. But in the final analysis, it is what the patient does in his or her day-to-day life that determines our success. The program outlined in this book, indeed, the book itself, is part of our continuing effort to educate the public about hypertension and to help individuals become more informed partners in their own health care.

Ray W. Gifford, Jr., M.D.
Chairman, Department of
Hypertension and Nephrology;
Vice Chairman, Division of
Nephrology; The Cleveland Clinic
Foundation

Glossary

ACTH. Adrenocorticotropic hormone, secreted by the pituitary gland and influences function of adrenal and other glands.

ALDOSTERONE. A steroid hormone that is released by the adrenal glands and promotes the body's conservation of salt and water and thereby raises blood pressure.

ALPHA ADRENERGIC BLOCKER. Drug that lowers blood pressure by blocking alpha receptor impulses of the sympathetic nervous system.

ANEURYSM. A weakened portion of blood vessel wall, resulting in a ballooning outward.

ANGINA PECTORIS. Chest pain caused by a temporary lack of oxygen to a portion of heart muscle. The condition is usually caused by coronary atherosclerosis, or chronic narrowing of the arteries. It can also be caused by low oxygen levels in the blood, restricted blood flow to the heart, coronary spasm, or overexertion.

ANGIOTENSIN. A substance produced in response to release of renin by kidneys and one of the body's most potent vasoconstrictors, or substance that narrows blood vessels and raises blood pressure.

ANTIDIURETIC HORMONE. A hormone that stimulates smooth muscles of blood vessels to constrict, or narrow, thus raising blood pressure.

ANTIHYPERTENSIVE DRUGS. Drugs used to control hypertension, or high blood pressure.

AORTA. The main artery (leading away from the heart), which receives blood from the left ventricle of the heart. It arches over the heart and branches off to carry blood down through the chest and abdomen, while the carotid artery carries blood upward to the brain.

AORTIC STENOSIS. A narrowing of the aorta or of the aortic valve, the opening between the left ventricle of the heart and the aorta.

ARRHYTHMIA. A variation from the normal heart-rate rhythm.

ARTERIES. Blood vessels that carry blood away from the heart.

ARTERIOLES. The smallest of the arterial vessels (diameter 1/125 inch). Their function is to pass the blood from the arteries to the capillaries.

ARTERIOSCLEROSIS. A thickening and loss of elasticity of the artery walls, which cuts down on blood flow and strains the heart.

ATHEROSCLEROSIS. A type of arteriosclerosis in which, in addition to the thickening and reduced elasticity of the arteries, a fatty substance (plaque) forms on the inner walls of the arteries, narrowing them and obstructing the flow of blood.

ATRIUM. One of the two upper chambers of the heart. The right atrium receives unoxygenated blood from the body, and the left atrium receives oxygenated blood from the lungs ready for circulation.

AUTONOMIC NERVOUS SYSTEM. The involuntary nervous system, consisting of the sympathetic and the parasympathetic nerves, which regulate body tissue and function. The sympathetic nerves tend to increase heart rate, while the parasympathetic nerves tend to slow heart rate and lower blood pressure, when stimulated.

BARORECEPTORS. Nerve cells that detect fluctuations in blood pressure and act through the autonomic nervous system to stabilize blood pressure.

BASAL METABOLISM. The minimum amount of energy needed to maintain basic life functions, such as breathing, circulation, metabolism, digestion, etc.

BETA ADRENERGIC BLOCKER. A drug used to treat hypertension by blocking certain actions of the sympathetic nervous system.

BIOFEEDBACK. A behavior modification therapy by which a patient is taught to control involuntary body systems, such as blood pressure, through the visualization of body functions. The use of lights and projected images depicting normally involuntary functions have been highly successful in helping the patient control biological systems.

BLOOD PRESSURE. The force exerted by circulating blood against the artery walls. Blood pressure measurements reflect the systolic pressure, based on contraction, over the diastolic pressure, reflecting the relaxation of the heart. A typical blood pressure reading (in the normal range) might be 120/80.

BLOOD VOLUME. Amount of blood circulating in the body.

BRADYCARDIA. Abnormally slow heart rate.

CALCIUM CHANNEL BLOCKER. A drug that blocks some of the movement of calcium to vascular smooth muscles, thereby dilating blood vessels and lowering blood pressure.

CALORIE. A unit of energy representing the amount of heat required to raise the temperature of one kilogram of water one degree Celsius. Calories are used as a measurement of how much energy is present in foods.

CAPILLARIES. The smallest of all the blood vessels, which pass oxygen and nutrients to all body tissues while removing carbon dioxide and waste products.

CARDIAC OUTPUT. The amount of blood pumped by the heart per minute.

CAROTID ARTERIES. The principal arteries supplying blood to the head and neck, one on each side of the neck. Each has two branches, internal and external. The external carotid artery is close to the surface and may be used as a pulse point in measuring heart rate.

CAROTID SINUS. An area of the carotid artery, just above the division into branches, in which special nerve cells sense any change in blood pressure and respond by changing heart rate.

CATECHOLAMINES. Hormones such as dopamine, norepinephrine, and epinephrine that activate the fight-or-flight response; often referred to as stress hormones.

CATHETER. A thin, flexible tube that can be inserted deep into body organs for use in diagnosis, treatment, or drainage. A cardiac catheter is inserted into the heart, its progress watched on a fluoroscope, for use in diagnosis and treatment of heart and blood vessel disease.

CEREBROVASCULAR ACCIDENT. A stroke.

COARCTATION OF THE AORTA. Congenital narrowing of the aorta, resulting in upper body hypertension and weak or absent pulses in the lower body.

COLLATERAL CIRCULATION. A detouring of the blood through small vessels when a main blood vessel has been blocked off.

CONGESTIVE HEART FAILURE. Congestion in the body tissues caused by a failure of the heart to pump its normal amount of blood, leading to accumulation of fluid in the abdomen, legs, and/or lungs. This condition can develop over a period of years, although attacks can be short and severe. Common consequence of long-standing hypertension.

CONSTRICTION. Narrowing of blood vessels caused by contraction of smooth muscles in vessel walls.

COOMBS TEST. Blood test to determine whether red blood cells are coated with antibodies.

CORONARY ARTERIES. The arteries that conduct blood to the heart muscle, rising from the base of the aorta and coming down over the top of the heart like a crown, or corona.

CORONARY ATHEROSCLEROSIS. Known as coronary heart disease, this is a narrowing of the coronary arteries caused by thickening of the inner layer of the arterial walls (which reduces the blood supply to the heart muscle).

CORONARY HEART DISEASE. A narrowing of the coronary arteries leading to a decreased blood supply to the heart. Also known as coronary artery disease and ischemic heart disease.

CUSHING'S SYNDROME. Rare disease marked by excessive secretion of adrenal hormones. Symptoms include hypertension, accumulation of fat about the face and trunk, abnormal carbohydrate metabolism, menstrual irregularities, and hirsutism (abnormal hair growth).

DIASTOLE. The period of relaxation in each heartbeat.

DIASTOLIC BLOOD PRESSURE. The lower measurement in a blood pressure reading that reflects the pressure in the arteries when relaxed. The lower of the two numbers in a blood pressure reading.

DILATION. A widening or opening of blood vessels beyond the norm.

DIURESIS. Increased output of urine.

DIURETIC. A type of drug used to treat hypertension by promoting salt excretion and thereby removing excess body fluids.

DYSPNEA. Shortness of breath.

EDEMA. Abnormal accumulation of body fluid.

ELECTROCARDIOGRAM. Commonly known as EKG or ECG, this is a test which graphically records the electric currents generated by the heart. Results of the test reveal heart rate and certain abnormalities, such as undersupply of blood or enlargement of the heart chambers.

EPINEPHRINE. Also called adrenaline. Hormone secreted by the adrenal glands, situated just above the kidneys, which increases heart rate and constricts certain blood vessels while dilating others.

ESSENTIAL HYPERTENSION. High blood pressure of an unknown cause. Also called primary hypertension.

EXERCISE ELECTROCARDIOGRAM. Also called a stress test, this is administered while the patient is exercising, usually on a treadmill or an exercise bicycle, to record the electric currents generated by the heart in order to monitor heart functions.

GANGLION. A group of nerve cells located outside the brain and spinal cord.

GANGLIONIC BLOCKING AGENT. A drug that inhibits nerve impulses in the ganglia, and thereby lowers blood pressure.

HEART BLOCK. A blockage or slowing of the electrical impulse within the heart's conduction system, causing uncoordinated rhythms of the upper and lower heart chambers. This can be corrected with an artificial pacemaker.

HEART FAILURE. A condition in which the heart is unable to pump enough blood to maintain normal blood circulation. It may be due to circulatory disorder, high blood pressure, rheumatic heart disease, birth defect, or heart attack.

HEMOGLOBIN. The oxygen-carrying, red pigment of the red blood cells. Hemoglobin absorbs oxygen in the lungs, becoming bright red, and is then called oxyhemoglobin. After some of the oxygen has been distributed to body tissues, the hemoglobin turns dark burgundy and is called reduced hemoglobin.

HIRSUTISM Abnormal hair growth.

HYPERALDOSTERONISM. Excessive secretion of aldosterone, an adrenal steroid hormone, resulting in high blood pressure, potassium loss, weakness, and buildup of sodium and fluid.

HYPERCHOLESTEROLEMIA. An excess of cholesterol, a fat-like lipid, in the blood.

HYPERKALEMIA. An excess of potassium in the blood.

HYPERLIPOPROTEINEMIA. An excess of lipoproteins—complexes of fatty substances called lipids and certain proteins—in the blood.

HYPERTENSION. High blood pressure.

HYPERURICEMIA. An excess of uric acid in the blood, sometimes leading to or aggravating gout.

HYPERVOLEMIA. Abnormally high blood volume.

HYPOKALEMIA. A depletion of potassium in the blood. A side effect of some antihypertensive drugs.

HYPOTENSION. Low blood pressure.

HYPOVOLEMIA. Abnormally low blood volume.

HYPOXIA. Lack of oxygen in the organs and tissues of the body.

IDIOPATHIC. Of unknown causes, e.g., idiopathic hypertension.

ISCHEMIA. Temporary oxygen deficiency in a localized part of the body, caused by an obstruction in the blood vessel.

KOROTKOFF SOUNDS. Characteristic sounds that are heard through a stethoscope during blood pressure measurement.

LABILE HYPERTENSION. Blood pressure that is high at some times and normal at others.

LIPOPROTEIN. A complex of lipid and protein molecules bound together.

LOADING DOSE. An initial dose administered to achieve fast therapeutic effect.

MALIGNANT HYPERTENSION. Progressive hypertension that is usually due to kidney disease; a medical emergency.

MYOCARDIAL INFARCTION. A heart attack resulting in permanent damage, or death, of an area of the myocardium, or heart muscle.

NOREPINEPHRINE. Also called noradrenaline, this organic compound raises blood pressure by constricting the small blood vessels.

NORMOTENSIVE. Normal blood pressure.

ORTHOSTATIC HYPOTENSION. Dizziness or fainting upon standing up caused by a drop in blood pressure.

PALPITATION. An abnormal heart rate, indicated by a sensation of fluttering around the heart area.

PAPILLEDEMA. Accumulation of fluid in the optic disk, the area of the retina that adjoins the optic nerve. A symptom of high blood pressure.

PARASYMPATHETIC NERVOUS SYSTEM. Part of the autonomic nervous system that slows heart rate, reduces output of blood, and dilates blood vessels to lower blood pressure.

PHEOCHROMOCYTOMA. Development of a tumor of cells in the adrenal gland which secrete stress hormones and cause high blood pressure and other symptoms.

POSTURAL HYPOTENSION. Dizziness or fainting upon standing up caused by a drop in blood pressure.

POTASSIUM. Mineral found in many foods that is one of the body's essential electrolytes, needed to maintain proper biochemical balance. Also instrumental in muscle function and other body processes.

PREECLAMPSIA. A condition arising in the latter part of pregnancy, marked by fluid retention, high blood pressure, headaches, and visual disturbances. A medical emergency that threatens both mother and fetus.

PROSTAGLANDIN. A class of hormone-like substances produced by many body tissues that affect the nervous system, blood pressure, reproduction, metabolism, and numerous other body functions.

RENAL. Pertaining to the kidneys.

RENIN. An enzyme found in the kidney that is transformed by other body tissues into angiotensin, which raises blood pressure.

RENOVASCULAR HYPERTENSION. High blood pressure caused by diminished blood flow to a kidney, which prompts release of renin.

SCLEROSIS. Hardening or thickening, as in arteriosclerosis, or hardening of the arteries.

SECONDARY HYPERTENSION. High blood pressure caused by some other underlying disease.

SINUS RHYTHM. Normal heart rhythm initiated in the sinoatrial node, or pacemaker.

SODIUM. A mineral found in salt that is an essential electrolyte, needed to maintain fluid balance.

SPHYGMOMANOMETER. An instrument used for measuring blood pressure in the arteries.

STENOSIS. A narrowing of an opening, such as a valve.

SYMPATHETIC NERVOUS SYSTEM. The part of the autonomic nervous system that is stimulated by epinephrine.

SYNCOPE. The act of fainting, often caused by insufficient blood and oxygen to the brain.

SYSTOLE. The period of contraction of the heart in each heartbeat.

SYSTOLIC BLOOD PRESSURE. The upper reading of the blood pressure measurement that reflects the pressure in the artery when contracted.

TACHYCARDIA. Abnormally fast heart rate.

THIAZIDE DIURETICS. A class of drugs that increase excretion of sodium by the kidneys. Often used to treat hypertension and edema, excessive buildup of body fluid.

TRANSIENT ISCHEMIC ATTACKS. TIAs or ministrokes. Attacks of numbness, partial paralysis, speech difficulty, or other symptoms caused by temporary ischemia of localized areas of the brain. May signal an impending stroke.

VASOCONSTRICTOR. An impulse or agent that causes the muscles of the arterioles to constrict, raising blood pressure.

VASODILATOR. An impulse or agent that causes the muscles of the arterioles to relax, lowering blood pressure.

VASOPRESSOR. A substance that produces narrowing or constriction of blood vessels, thereby raising blood pressure.

VEIN. Blood vessel that carries blood from various parts of the body back to the heart. All veins except the pulmonary veins carry unoxygenated blood. The pulmonary veins carry freshly oxygenated blood from the lungs to the heart.

VENOUS BLOOD. Unoxygenated blood.

VENTRICLE. One of the two pumping chambers of the heart. The left ventricle pumps oxygenated blood through the arteries to the body tissues, while the right ventricle pumps unoxygenated blood through the pulmonary artery to the lungs for reoxygenation.

Index